Series / Number 07-073

UNDERSTANDING SIGNIFICANCE TESTING

LAWRENCE B. MOHR
The University of Michigan

SAGE PUBLICATIONS
The International Professional Publishers
Newbury Park   London   New Delhi

For information:

 Sage Publications, Inc.
2455 Teller Road
Thousand Oaks, California 91320
E-mail: order@sagepub.com

Sage Publications Ltd.
6 Bonhill Street
London EC2A 4PU
United Kingdom

Sage Publications India Pvt. Ltd.
M-32 Market
Greater Kailash I
New Delhi 110 048 India

Printed in the United States of America

Library of Congress Catalog Card No. 89-043409

ISBN 0-8039-3568-4

00   01   02   03   04   10   9

When citing a university paper, please use the proper form. Remember to cite the Sage University Paper series title and include paper number. One of the following formats can be adapted (depending on the style manual used):

(1) MOHR, L. B. (1990). *Understanding Significance Testing*. Sage University Paper series on Quantitative Applications in the Social Sciences, 07-073. Newbury Park, CA: Sage.

OR

(2) Mohr, L. B. (1990). *Understanding significance testing.* (Sage University Paper series on Quantitative Applications in the Social Sciences, 07-073). Newbury Park, CA: Sage.

CONTENTS

Acknowledgments   4

Series Editor's Introduction   5

1. Introduction   7

2. Some Definitions   9

3. The Sampling Distribution   13
   Frequency Distributions   14
   The Unit of Analysis   16
   The Distribution of a Statistic   18
   Mathematical Sampling Distributions   19
   The Normal Curve   21
   The Sampling Distribution of the Mean   22
   The Task   25

4. Interval Estimation   28
   Seven Steps to Interval Estimation for the
      Population Mean   28
   Seven Steps, Using the Z Distribution   38
   Seven Steps, Using the t Distribution   42
   Conclusion   47

5. Significance Testing   49
   The Indirect or Interval-Estimation Method   51
   The Direct Method of Significance Testing   54
   The Textbook versus the Informal Approach   60
   Type II Error   61
   One-Tailed Tests   64

6. The Functions of the Test   67

References   75

About the Author   76

ACKNOWLEDGMENTS

I am most grateful for support and comments from Elizabeth M. Hawthorne, George Julnes, and the series editor and an anonymous reviewer from Sage Publications.

I am grateful to the Library Executor of the late Sir Ronald A. Fisher, FRS, to Dr. Frank Yates, RFS, and the Longman Group Ltd., London for permission to reprint Table 3 from their book, *Statistical Tables for Biological, Agricultural and Medical Research* (6th ed.) 1974.

SERIES EDITOR'S INTRODUCTION

In the quantitative analysis of social science data, significance testing is the most used, and arguably the most useful, of all techniques. Regardless of the discipline — anthropology, economics, education, political science, psychology, sociology — the application of significance tests provides a standard first cut at the research hypotheses. From the results, the researcher is encouraged to pursue certain theories, and to discard others. On the one hand, when the relationship between X and Y is "significant at .05," the notion that X is somehow important for Y gains critical support. On the other hand, if that relationship does not test significant (at .05 or another conventional level), the likely conclusion is that X is not important for Y. Few hypotheses, in other words, survive and prosper if they fail an initial test of significance.

Take the example of Professor Brown, an educational psychologist exploring the predictors of academic achievement. One hypothesis is that student homework effort relates to classroom performance. From her survey of 100 college students, she correlates homework hours per week with grade-point average, yielding an $r = .35$. She applies a significance test (.05, two-tails) to the correlation, which it passes. Brown concludes that homework is most likely related to grades at her university. What does this conclusion mean exactly? To what extent is it justified? Such questions, along with many others, are answered in this splendid monograph.

As the title implies, Professor Mohr seeks to impart an "understanding" of significance testing, rather than a mere "cookbook" set of rules. Systematic explanations are developed with the tools of clear language and elementary math. First, basic terms, such as *variance, standard deviation*, and *parameter*, are meaningfully defined. Then, the vital concepts of random sampling and the sampling distribution unfold. With that perspective, "interval" and "point" estimation approaches receive rich consideration. In particular, the complementarities between confidence interval construction and ordinary significance testing are laid bare.

6

Moreover, numerous central issues surrounding significance testing are evaluated, among them Type I vs. Type II error, one-tailed vs. two-tailed tests, factors affecting significance, causality, and strength-of-relationship. Throughout, the explication is lucid, without sacrificing rigor. Readers at all levels of research experience, from the first-semester student to the seasoned practitioner, stand to profit from Professor Mohr's introduction to this most fundamental topic.

— Michael S. Lewis-Beck
Series Editor

UNDERSTANDING SIGNIFICANCE TESTING

LAWRENCE B. MOHR
The University of Michigan

1. INTRODUCTION

Significance tests are extremely common in social science research. Many people would say that they are entirely too common, and there are two basic reasons for that claim. The first is that the tests do not provide enough information, and the second is that the situations in which they are truly and legitimately applicable are less frequently encountered in social science than one might think. There is some truth in both of these bases for the claim, but not enough, I think, to make us abandon significance testing or put less effort into teaching and learning about it than we do. I will postpone treating the second of the two reasons until the very end. The first — that the tests do not provide enough information — will pop up in several places, and I think that a few words about it are in order right at the beginning.

A significance test is a test of a hypothesis; for example, the hypothesis that a certain population correlation is zero or that a certain population mean is 37.5. There is an alternative to testing such hypotheses, based on the same statistical reasoning, that in many cases would give more valuable information. Instead of testing such a specific, exact hypothesis, one can fashion an estimate of what the value in question really is. One can find, for example, that the magnitude of the focal relationship in a population is probably 0.6 ± 0.3 ("0.6 plus or minus 0.3," that is, a magnitude between 0.3 and 0.9), or perhaps 0.3 ± 0.6. In so doing, one may also be taken as testing an exact hypothesis, but by an indirect route; the first of the two interval estimates just mentioned, for example, would lead you to reject the hypothesis that the relationship is exactly zero, whereas the second one would not. But you obviously know more than just enough for a simple decision about rejecting a hypothesis when you also have the probable range in which the relationship actually does lie. For that reason, many would advocate interval estimation of this sort (commonly called "confidence inter-

8

vals") in place of significance testing. However, significance testing is far more common. Why?

There are probably many reasons, but the main one, I think, is that significance tests really do satisfy the goals of social scientists more frequently than do interval estimates. We are in most cases not far enough along theoretically to be concerned with the range in which an estimated value probably lies; we just want to know whether or not a certain relationship or other quantity is worth further thought — whether it might repay additional research effort. If the relationship, insofar as we have been able to observe or estimate, is zero or close to it, then it may not merit further exploration, especially in competition with other ideas. If we are looking at only one such relationship, then perhaps we would get the most for our time and trouble out of an interval estimate, but we may and often do consider hundreds of them. Instead of examining a welter of interval estimates, involving many more numbers in most cases than we have any desire to think about, we simply look at a list of essentially qualitative results — "significant" or "nonsignificant," that is, "perhaps worth more thought" or "probably not." (This rule would rarely be followed slavishly; there are always cases in which one would distribute further effort on the basis of other considerations, as well.)

Clearly, though, the interval estimate provides so much information that it also has a great deal to recommend it. Both procedures are important, and both should be learned. Since they are based on what is at bottom the same statistical reasoning, although this is not always apparent to the newcomer, it can also be quite efficient to learn both. Then the question becomes: Which should be learned first? My experience suggests that the logic of interval estimation is less tortuous and more appealing. Furthermore, interval estimation may be seen to encompass significance testing, but the reverse is not true. The statistical reasoning behind both is generally referred to as "classical statistical inference." In this monograph, we will approach classical inference mainly by the path of interval estimation, adding direct significance testing as a special twist. But I will also, at the end, cover the uses and misuses of significance testing in itself because it is both so common and so controversial a procedure.

Before continuing, it is also important to say a word about the function of classical inference. When we speak of classical inference, just what is it that we are inferring? Basically, it is one of two things. The first, as the above examples suggest, is that we infer something about the characteristics of an unobserved population on the basis of the characteristics of an observed sample from that population. For example, if a sample relation measures 0.6, we might infer that the population relation is, with high probability, 0.6 ± 0.3 (confidence interval), or at least that the population relation is probably not zero (significance test). The second kind of inference, which comes into play primarily when an experimenter has implemented a randomized, controlled experiment, is to infer that a relation is probably *causal*, or that an instance of causation has probably taken place. Most of the rest of this monograph will deal with the first sort of inference; in the concluding section, in the context of the uses of significance testing, I will add the reasoning necessary to understand the second, or causal, sort of inference.

2. SOME DEFINITIONS

I assume that the reader is familiar with such basic quantitative terms as percentage and proportion. A large number of additional concepts will be introduced and defined as we go along. In fact, understanding significance testing may largely be seen as coming to understand the meanings of a few dozen special terms.

At the outset, it is necessary to cover a number of basic concepts. The first is a *variable. A variable is a property of individuals that may take on two or more "values," or scores, but not at the same time for the same individual.* For example, "Sex" is a property of individuals that may take either the value "male" or the value "female." "Ease of understanding" is a property of individuals that, in a study of innovations (so that each "individual" is one innovation), might be able to take the values "easy," "moderately difficult," or "difficult." "Expenditures" is a property of individuals that, in a study of cities (so that each individual is one city), might take on such values as $1.3 million, $2.1 million, and so on. Note that "individuals" in this context may be people and they may be inanimate objects or other entities, such as innovations. Also, they may be single ideas, objects, or organisms, such as individual people or individual innovations, but they may also be collectivities, such as cities. In the latter sort of case, the collectivities are thought of as individuals because many of them are being considered in a single study and each one is taken as a whole, or as a unit. Examples of such collectivities are classes in a school, forests in the western United States, and countries in the United Nations.

The reader has probably studied beginning statistics, but the concepts of mean, variance, and standard deviation are so important for understanding classical inference that a very brief review of them will be prudent. These three concepts become relevant as summarizers of scores on a variable when those scores are quantitative, that is, when we deal with variables like expenditures rather than gender (I skip lightly here over what can be a highly technical subject; the reader is referred to the chapters on scales of measurement in most beginning statistics books for a basic treatment and references).

A *mean*, or an arithmetic mean, is of course a synonym for an average, as commonly understood. To arrive at it, one simply adds up all the scores and divides by N, the number of such scores.

Variances and *standard deviations* are a bit more complicated. Instead of giving information about the midpoint of a set of scores, they convey information about the spread of those scores *around* their mean. These summarizers help us to make quick distinctions between some sets of scores that are closely clumped together and others that are spread out quite widely. The best measure for accomplishing this in an intuitively clear fashion is neither the standard deviation nor the variance, but the "average absolute deviation": (1) Subtract the mean from each score in order to get the distance of that score from the mean, (2) consider all of these distances or deviations from the mean as positive (otherwise, if you added them up you would always get zero), and (3) take the average of these positive or "absolute" deviations. For example, if we had the scores 4, 5, and 6 inches, the mean would be 5 inches. The deviations would be −1 inch, 0, and 1 inch, respectively. Changing these to absolute values gives 1, 0, and 1. The mean of these three numbers is 0.667 inches. To say that the average absolute deviation here is 0.667 is to say that each of the three scores is an average of 0.667 inches away from the original mean of 5 inches. This tells us something. For example, if the three scores were 1, 5, and 9 inches, the average absolute deviation would be 2.667 inches. The second set of scores is clearly more spread out around its mean than the first one. In fact, if we want to know dispersion, or "spread-outness," it is hard to think of a clearer way to think about the concept than in terms of the average distance of the various scores from their mean, recognizing that some are generally nearby and some farther away.

As it happens, however, clarity and simplicity are not the only concerns in developing such summary measures. Another kind of consideration is mathematical utility and connectedness. The variance and standard deviation are also measures of dispersion, and they score extremely well on this other, more mathematical dimension. At the same time, the average absolute deviation is quite pathetic in this perspective; it connects mathematically with practically nothing. Which should be used? If the contest were only between the average absolute deviation and the variance, the race might be close, because the variance provides very little information intuitively about dispersion. Instead of being an average *absolute* deviation, *the variance is the average squared deviation from the mean.* For the numbers 1, 5, and 9, the variance is $[(-4)^2 + (0)^2 + (4)^2]/3 = 32/3 = 10.667$ inches. What possible information can this quantity convey about the numbers 1, 5, and 9? None at all! Thus, although the variance clearly dominates the average absolute deviation in mathematical utility, just the reverse is true with respect to intuitive meaningfulness.

But let us move on to the *standard deviation.* This measure is simply the square root of the variance. It cannot be arrived at in any other way and has no *intrinsic* meaning other than as the square root of the variance. It is not, for example, the average of anything. For almost all sets of scores that we deal with, however, the standard deviation turns out to be reasonably close in magnitude to the average absolute deviation! In fact, it will generally be a little larger, the average absolute deviation being about four-fifths as great as the standard deviation (the standard deviation of the scores 1, 5, and 9 inches is 3.27 inches, as compared to the average absolute deviation of 2.667). Thus, the standard deviation has the great advantage of mathematical connectedness and, by being a rough guide to the average distance of a number of scores from their mean, it also tells us almost exactly what we want to know intuitively about dispersion. The standard deviation, then, is the summary measure of choice for this purpose (there are others, but none so commonly used.) The variance is used frequently as well, but more because of its mathematical convenience and relation to the standard deviation than for any intrinsic communicative value.

The remaining concepts that we need at the beginning make a pair: *statistic* and *parameter. A statistic is a summarizing property of a collectivity when that collectivity is considered to be a sample.* The term has other uses and meanings, many of which will also arise in this monograph, but this is a particular, technical meaning that will be of great importance. I will try to be sure that it is always clear when "statistic" is being used in this technical sense. The word to note most carefully in the above definition is "sample." It is highly restrictive, since it turns out that in a great deal of quantitative work we either do not deal with samples at all or do not consider them in their true statistical role of representatives of a larger population. Statisticians rarely break the rule of using "statistics" to refer only to samples, but practicing scientists frequently do, to the great disadvantage of those who need to understand just what is being accomplished in research. The "collectivity" referred to in the definition is, of course, composed of individuals of some sort, and those individuals have scores on one or more variables. For example, the collectivity might be a sample of children from a school, and each child might have been given a score on the variable, "father's income." An example of a statistic, then, would be the average father's income of the children in the sample, or the median father's income, or the maximum father's income, the variance in father's income, and so forth. A statistic may also summarize the relations among several variables, still all in one quantity: for example, the multiple correlation coefficient denoting the accuracy with which (1) the school performance of children in the sample may be predicted from (2) father's income and (3) birth order (only child, first child, second child, etc.). In this monograph, by the way, the term "sample" will refer to a random sample. It is not that nonrandom samples are "bad," but simply that classical inference is in principle irrelevant to sampling that is not rooted somehow in a random procedure.

A parameter is a summarizing property of a collectivity when that collectivity is not *considered to be a sample.* The collectivity might be a population from which a sample is drawn; or it might just be a group (large or small) that is considered, at least at the moment, for its own sake; or it might be a hypothetical population, such as the infinite population to which a true, universal causal law applies.

The distinction between a statistic and a parameter is important for classical inference because what is generally involved there is an inference about a population parameter on the basis of a sample statistic. For that reason, we need to have and do have notation that serves to keep the two distinct, so that we may always know what sort of thing we are talking about. In most cases, a parameter is symbolized by a Greek letter, and the corresponding statistic is symbolized by the corresponding Roman letter usually italicized. For example, a standard deviation in parameter notation is written as "σ," whereas in statistic notation it is written as "*s*." Similarly, the regression slope coefficient is written as β for parameter, and "*b*" for the corresponding statistic. The convention does not always hold, however. In particular, the population mean of X or Y is symbolized as μ_X or μ_Y whereas the sample mean is given by $\overline{X}$ or $\overline{Y}$, pronounced "X-bar," "Y-bar."

So much for introductory comments and definitions. We turn now to the all-important notion of a sampling distribution.

3. THE SAMPLING DISTRIBUTION

The idea of the sampling distribution is fundamental to an understanding of classical inference. It is the keystone of the entire process; without clarity in regard to the sampling distribution, only a muddy and confused notion of significance testing and confidence intervals is possible. Furthermore, it is a difficult idea to grasp. The student should not suppose that he or she is expected to assimilate the material on this topic in one quick reading. On the contrary, it seems for most people to take careful and repeated study, probably because the concept is a strange one from the standpoint of ordinary experience.

Roughly speaking, the sampling distribution functions in the following way: The basic task in classical inference, as noted above, is to learn something about an unobserved population on the basis of an observed sample. More specifically, it is to learn something about a population parameter on the basis of a sample statistic. Not much of this task can be accomplished directly. Let us say that the sample yields a correlation of 0.43. All we can say directly from there about the population from which the sample was drawn is "My best guess is that the corresponding correlation in the population is also 0.43." That is fine as far as it goes, but it generally does not go far enough. One would often have quite an insecure feeling about a guess of that nature because one would not know how much confidence to put in it or how accurate it is likely to be. To add these sorts of dimensions to our statements about the unobserved population, the sample itself is not enough. We will see that the sampling distribution is the extra tool that is necessary. It forms a kind of bridge between the sample and the population. In the sampling distribution, certain bits of information about the sample and the population come together in such a way that one can make the desired statements about population parameters with varying degrees of confidence and with varying degrees of accuracy. As the reader might guess, great accuracy and great confidence do not go together; one must be traded off for the other, and all of that is accomplished within the mediating or bridging context of the sampling distribution.

Frequency Distributions

A sampling distribution is a type of frequency distribution, and so it is first necessary to understand the latter term. *A frequency distribution is a depiction of the number of times each value of a variable occurs in a sample or population.* Very often, a frequency distribution is referred to simply as a "distribution"; the two terms are essentially synonomous. The depiction mentioned in the definition might be just a series of numbers, as in Male: 42; Female: 39, meaning that there were 42 males and 39 females in the collectivity. Sometimes the frequencies are depicted by means of a bar graph or a pie chart. Often, the frequency distribution is given by a curve rising above a horizontal axis, such that the height of the curve above a point on the axis depicts the number of times the score represented by that point occurs in the collectivity. In an ordinary bell-shaped curve, for example, the scores in the middle of the axis occur most frequently, while those toward the ends occur least frequently, as one can quickly tell by the shape of the curve. It is possible also, and we will take advantage of this variant, to let the height of the curve represent *relative* frequency instead of simple frequency. The relative frequency is the *proportion* of times a value occurs, rather than the number. For example, for the distribution of the variable "sex" in the illustration just offered, the relative frequencies of Male and Female are 52% and 48%, respectively. Thus, the sum of all the relative frequencies in a single distribution is always equal to 1.0, or 100% of the cases.

If the divisions or points along the horizontal axis are infinitely small because any decimal is possible, a score cannot accurately be represented by a true, physical point. In that instance, a better way to think of the whole is as 100% of the area under the curve, rather than 100% of the cases. Moreover, a score must then technically be considered as a small interval, or neighborhood of scores, along the line, and its relative frequency as the proportion of the area occupied by the bar rising above that interval, rather than the infinitely thin bar rising above a point (see figure 3.1).

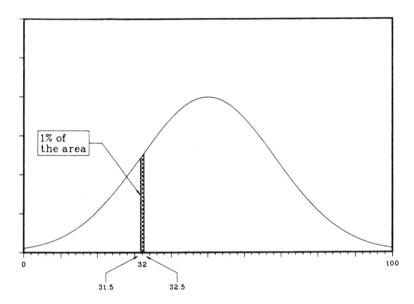

Figure 3.1. Infinitely Divided Number Line

It is important to keep in mind that a frequency distribution always has two components. One component is the scores on the variable concerned, such as Male-Female, High-Medium-Low, or all of the possible numbers and fractions between, say, 0 and 20. When the distribution is given as a curve over an axis, these scores are ranged along the axis. The other component is the frequency (or relative frequency) of each score, given by the height of the curve above each relevant point. Sometimes, people make the mistake of thinking of a distribution as those scores on a variable that happen to occur in a particular sample or population, forgetting about the other component that gives the number or proportion of times each such score occurs, that is, the number or proportion of cases represented by each score. If we say without further clarification that a distribution is "infinite," the statement is ambiguous with respect to component; it could mean that the axis stretches out to plus or minus infinity along the number line, and it could also mean that there is an infinite number of cases or individuals in the collectivity (even if the range of scores is finite). Or, it could mean both of these things.

The Unit of Analysis

There is one more concept to introduce before we can come to grips with the sampling distribution. *The unit of analysis is the kind of individual described by a variable or set of variables.* It is unfortunately not always clear what the unit of analysis is, and unless the investigator gives us this information directly, we must do the best we can to glean it by thinking about the variables employed and the sorts of entities they describe. The unit of analysis may be people, and it very often is in social research. It may also be unmarried women, or U.S. voters, or innovations, or forests, trees, or cities. If the variable is height, with such scores as 50 feet, 125 feet, and so forth, the unit of analysis may be trees, but if the variable is *average* height (of trees), the unit of analysis is clearly a *group* of trees, something like a forest, or a grove, which means that many such groups are apparently under consideration in one study (or else the *average* of something would not be a *variable*).

If we are talking about a relationship, in which one or more variables are being considered as determinants of another one, all of the variables must be descriptors of the same unit of analysis. It is sometimes difficult to be certain of one's *own* unit of analysis when thinking about a relation or set of relations in a potential study. Confusion can reign when all variables being considered do not apply to the same unit of analysis and the investigator fails to recognize this. One might reasonably think, for example, that interest groups are influential in determining the adoption of policies to the extent that they have access to relevant governmental officials, and that the success of proposed policies in gaining adoption reflects the influence of rich and powerful interest groups more than any other groups in society. Here we have what might seem to be one integrated theory, but two analyses, or two different studies, or at least a study in two analytic stages. In the first, the unit of analysis is the interest group, and the two variables involved are the extent of access of each group and its (average) degree of influence over policy adoption. In the second, the unit of analysis is the policy proposal, and the variables are the degree of success of each and the (average) degree of wealth/power of its supporting groups. Because the two units of analysis are different, the first and last studies cannot be *statistically* combined. Similarly, one might think that organizations with more technical expertise than others adopt innovations faster, and that the kinds of innovations that take the most time to diffuse through a population of organizations are those that demand the most technical expertise. Again, there would seem to be one general subject being discussed here, but what is in reality reflected is two studies. The first is a study of organizations: the greater their technical expertise, the earlier they adopt. The second is a study of innovations: the more technical expertise they demand, the slower they diffuse. I cannot provide a set of rules for determining what the unit of analysis is or should be; I can only urge that the reader think about this issue in all cases and make a point of puzzling out what the various variables describe. Technical expertise and earliness of adoption describe organizations; technical expertise required and diffusion time, however, describe innovations. A good approach to almost any but the simplest study is "First, just what is the unit of analysis here?"

For our purposes, the unit of analysis is critical because the sampling distribution is a special kind of frequency distribution, special in that it has a unique unit of analysis. The unit of analysis is not the person, or the innovation, or the tree. It is a collectivity. But it is not an ordinary collectivity, either; it does not come in bunches such that a large number of the collectivities is observed in a given study, such as classes in school, or forests, or Congressional delegations. It is a special collectivity: the sample. But in most studies, only one sample is observed; how can the sample be an "individual," that is, one of many such individuals represented in a distribution? We will see that in a moment. First recognize, however, that the variables that describe this unit of analysis must also be special. Since a variable is a description of an individual, what is that description when the individual is a sample? The answer is "a statistic." Thus, "The mean diffusion time in this sample of innovations I have selected is eight months," or "The mean family income for the census tract in this sample of census tracts is $20,000," or "The correlation (a statistic) between need for achievement and grade-point average in this sample of sophomores is 0.55." Clearly, if there were a lot of *samples* of innovations, or of census tracts, or of sophomores, in a study (which there almost never are), each of the samples could be characterized by a different score for mean diffusion time, or mean tract income, or correlation between need for achievement and grade-point average. Thus, in this very special and apparently nonreal sense, a statistic can be a variable, and can have a distribution.

The Distribution of a Statistic

What can possibly be meant, then, by this idea of a sampling distribution, or the distribution of a statistic? It is this. Think of a situation in which you are about to draw a sample from a population. You have numbered each individual in the population (that is, each person, voter, tree, forest, etc.), and you are about to draw some numbers from an urn, or read random numbers from a table, in order to take a random sample of a certain size from your population. At that moment, it is possible for you to have in mind a statistic that you will calculate once you have drawn the sample and made your measurements. For example, you may have in mind that you will measure intelligence by means of an IQ test and then calculate the mean intelligence (your statistic) of the individuals in the sample. Of course, the mean that you will find depends on the individuals who happen to fall into your sample. One sample would yield one mean intelligence, another might yield a different mean, and a third might yield the same as the first would have yielded even though it involved a different set of individuals.

At that moment, then, before you sample, there is a host of possibilities for the outcome of the statistic. *It is these possibilities for the resulting calculated statistic that are ranged along the horizontal axis of a sampling distribution.* That is why the statistic (e.g., the mean) can be a variable and the unit of analysis can be a sample even though there is only one sample in the study; it is because at the time when you establish the sampling distribution there is actually no sample at all, and the distribution is merely hypothetical — a distribution of possibilities. Note that the numbers ranged along the horizontal axis in your sampling situation would be different if you were going to calculate a different statistic — the median intelligence, for example, or the variance of the individual intelligence scores in the sample, or the correlation between intelligence and parents' income — and they would also be different if the population were a different group. Thus, a sampling distribution is not just one entity, but there may be any number of them, even in just the matter of the numbers ranged along the horizontal axis, depending on such things as the statistic and population we are talking about.

Furthermore, that is only one component. In addition to the numbers along the axis, there is also the matter of the number of times each such value occurs. In the case of the sampling distribution, of course, these calculated values do not in principle occur at all; they are merely possibilities. But what is meant here by "all the possibilities" is to think of continuing to draw samples of that same size forever and writing down the mean (or other statistic) that is calculated each time. In that case, the same sample might be drawn over and over again; furthermore, the same number might come up repeatedly, even if the same exact sample is not imagined as being repeated, simply because two or more different samples can have the same mean. Thus, the sampling distribution is infinite in its second component (whatever it may be in its first component); there is no end to the number of samples it includes. Clearly, though, some numbers are more probable than others; that is, in the sort of hypothetical situation we are visualizing, some numbers would come up more often than others. Still, since the number of individual samples in the sampling distribution is infinite, there is no sense in trying to have the second component be frequency itself. Even though some means occur more frequently than others, no mean occurs an exact number of times in an infinite collection of means. We can, however, think in terms of relative frequency or probability, and that is exactly what we do. In the long-run situation, some numbers result two or three times or one and a half times as often as others, or (to be more faithful to this hypothetical situation in which no numbers have resulted at all) some outcomes are more *probable* than others. Which are the most and least probable depends on such things as the nature of the population and the size of the hypothetical sample.

A sampling distribution is therefore a compendium of the probabilities of calculated outcomes when one is about to draw a sample of size n from a certain population and calculate a certain statistic. Examples of sampling distributions will be shown many times in the pages that follow, but there is no point in providing a picture now; we need to base it on more specific information. Still, given that this concept is probably the most important one in the monograph and that it is generally found to be a difficult one to master — even if it seems easy at first glance — the reader is advised to go over the above section more than once, if necessary, to achieve clarity on the meaning of a sampling distribution in the abstract.

Mathematical Sampling Distributions

It would not be surprising if a certain question were now puzzling the reader a great deal. "How is it possible that a hypothetical distribution like the sampling distribution can be so important and useful? If it is only a distribution of possibilities, it is not likely to be very concrete;

we may not even know what the various outcomes are and what may be their respective probabilities." But of course we can know, in the same sense that we can know what the possible outcomes are when we roll two dice, and how probable each of the various outcomes actually is. If we know a lot of relevant facts about the population from which a sample is to be drawn at random, then we may deduce quite a bit about the outcomes of the sampling process. For example, if we know how many people in the population have each IQ score, then we automatically know which scores are more and which are less probable when selecting strictly at random (just as we know that the numbers on a die are *equally* probable because in that case there is exactly one of each), and therefore which *mean* IQ scores are more and less likely to result. In fact, there is not even a need to have such exact and detailed information about the population. Such is the science of mathematics in regard to probability that we can actually know quite a bit about certain sampling distributions on the basis of only some rough, summary information about the population from which a sample is about to be drawn (and a good thing, too, because if we already had detailed information about the population there would obviously be no need to take a sample).

Before continuing, let us pause to appreciate how important the random sampling procedure is to classical inference. The sampling distribution is the foundation of all, but if we did not use some sort of random sampling procedure, then the specifics of the sampling distribution would be anybody's guess. What if I were to sample using the technique: "Pick any individual to start, look that selection over, then pick others in the population by looking them over, too, and trying your best to balance things out"? Or perhaps I might use another technique: "Given that the individuals in this population are widely scattered and that the sample has to be observed and measured, pick a sample in such a way that travel time to make those observations will be reasonably small." These are not necessarily "bad" sampling procedures; it is just that the rules of probability do not apply to them so as to yield a predetermined sampling distribution. Who can tell ahead of time what the results of such sampling procedures will be? The predetermined sampling distribution is simply irrelevant to such procedures, and so, therefore, is the entire edifice of classical inference. Thus, everything we say from now on assumes a random sampling procedure, or something close enough to it that an investigator and his or her audience are willing to consider it as amounting to the same thing.

The Normal Curve

Predetermined sampling distributions, which we will refer to simply as "sampling distributions" from now on, are given by mathematical formulas. The normal distribution is a curve defined by a certain formula and many statistics are found to have a sampling distribution that is normal. (I have now begun to write conversationally about the sampling distributions of different statistics, as though the idea were second nature. If it is not, then it would be best for the reader to stop and back up a bit.) The t distribution is another curve, defined by a different formula, and many statistics are found to have a sampling distribution that is the t distribution. Many people believe that the normal curve means simply a bell-shaped curve. That is incorrect. The t distribution is also a bell-shaped curve, looking so much like a normal curve that the two are essentially indistinguishable to the eye, yet it has a totally different formula. The formula I am speaking of in each case is the formula that, given a certain score on the horizontal axis, yields the height of the curve above that point. For both the normal distribution and the t distribution, the formula yields a curve that is bell-shaped, symmetrical around its mean, tapering into its tails, and asymptotic to the horizontal axis, that is, coming closer and closer but never actually touching the axis — never dropping to zero probability.

The normal curve was not simply discovered; it was approached by mathematicians gradually over a period of a great many years, largely in conjunction with trying to figure out the sampling distribution of the mean. You could not arrive at this result empirically (that is, by taking millions of samples and plotting their means) because the second component of a sampling distribution is infinite. Since it never ends, it never settles down in such a way that you can reach a conclusion about the exact shape that is taken by the lineup of probabilities. If you flip a fair coin a billion times, it doesn't necessarily come out half a billion heads, and, even if it did, ten more flips might spoil the 50-50 split. Although empirically the distribution definitely seems to tend towards half and half, the truth is that it comes out however it comes out. We simply have to make our definitions and formulas such that a fair coin is one that comes out half and half "in the long run." It is the same with the sampling distribution of the mean and the normal curve. The relation between the two is largely a matter of great mathematical convenience coupled with great empirical plausibility. From the normal curve as a beginning point, however, all of the other major curves used in classical statistical inference follow mathematically; the t distribution, the chi-square distribution, and the F distribution are all curves that specify the sampling distributions of a number of different statistics, and all are based on the normal distribution. The whole makes a remarkable, close-knit family that is wonderful in mathematical elegance and momentous in practical utility.

The Sampling Distribution of the Mean

Consider a large population of individuals about whom little is known in detail. We would like to learn as much as we can about what some of those details are, but we cannot undergo the expense of doing so by direct observation. Consider, for example, that this is the population of individual, noninstitutionalized Americans over 18 and that we wish to know their mean tolerance of the views of others. We have an instrument to measure tolerance on a scale of 0 to 100. We call this tolerance variable X. The population mean tolerance (a parameter) that is at present unknown we will symbolize by the notation μ_X, and the population standard deviation, another unknown parameter, we will symbolize by σ_X.

We might draw a random sample of size 500 from this population. In fact, there are organizations such as the Survey Research Center at the University of Michigan, the National Opinion Research Center at the University of Chicago, and others that have the capability of drawing such national samples and regularly do so. The samples are not strictly random samples, but they have a vital core of random selection that makes the notion of a sampling distribution relevant to them. Let us therefore continue to think of our samples as random.

As the sample is about to be drawn, and given that we are interested in calculating the sample mean tolerance, $\bar{X}$, there exists conceptually a sampling distribution of $\bar{X}$. That is, there are specific values that the sample mean tolerance $\bar{X}$ can take, and each such value has a probability, some greater, some less. It has been shown mathematically, summarized in a device called the Central Limit Theorem, that this distribution is approximately normal. Furthermore, the mean of the sampling distribution of $\bar{X}$, which would be symbolized as $\mu_{\bar{X}}$, is μ_X, in our case, the unknown mean tolerance in the population. This is a wonderfully convenient result. It means that, *on the average*, a sample mean tolerance is the same as the population mean tolerance. Note that the term "on the average" in the last sentence is a reference to this hypothetical distribution, this distribution of possibilities, that we call the sampling distribution of the mean; μ_X is the average of the infinite iterations of the possibilities for $\overline{X}$.

The Central Limit Theorem also tells us that the standard deviation of the sampling distribution of $\overline{X}$, which would be symbolized as $\sigma_{\overline{X}}$, is $\sigma_X/\sqrt{n}$, that is, the population standard deviation divided by the square root of the sample size. The standard deviation of the sampling distribution of any statistic has a special name that has become conventional. It is called the "standard error" of the statistic. Thus, we are now talking about the standard error of the mean. Whenever the term "standard error" is used instead of "standard deviation," the distribution referred to is a sampling distribution.

In sum, the Central Limit Theorem tells us (1) that the sampling distribution of $\overline{X}$ is normal, (2) that it has a certain mean, and (3) that it has a certain standard deviation. Why do we care about this information? It is intuitively plausible that we would feel we want to know $\overline{X}$ itself because it is so reasonable to use it to get an idea of the unknown population mean. The fact that the *average* $\overline{X}$ (the mean of the sampling distribution) is that very population mean is then a welcome and pleasing characteristic of the sampling distribution. For this piece of information, we are grateful to the Central Limit Theorem. It is not so intuitively clear why it would be important for us to know the other two pieces: that the sampling distribution is normal and that it has a standard deviation of a certain size. These latter two facts are not used directly to get an idea of the population mean, it is true; however, they will be a great help because they will enable us to figure out approximately how far off from the population mean (the target) our actual sample mean, when we draw it, is likely to be. Let us consider these two bits of information further.

To say that the sampling distribution of $\overline{X}$ is *normal* around the mean μ_X is rather a remarkable revelation. We did not stipulate that the population tolerance scores themselves must have a normal distribution. That distribution could in fact be lopsided in any fashion. Yet the sampling distribution is approximately normal about μ_X even so, as long as the sample size is large. Why is that so? It is because, whenever you draw a large sample, say 100 or more, from a population, that sample will tend to mirror the population itself. That is what random selection is all about. The sample will not always reflect the population exactly, of course, and sometimes it may look quite different. But large random samples generally are pretty representative. That implies that of all the possibilities for $\overline{X}$, those that are most probable are the ones that are close to $\mu_{\overline{X}}$. Furthermore, there is no more reason for them to be off on the high side than the low side, no matter what sort of lopsidedness the population shows. The reason is this: A mean is the center of gravity of a population of scores, meaning that there is just as much weight on either side of it. Therefore, if there are more actual people on one side of the population mean, say the low side, then balance must be achieved by the high scores being on average more extreme, or further away from the middle — what you might quite precisely call the teeter-totter principle. Any large random sample from such a population will tend to have a similar balance — more individuals with low scores, but high scorers that are more extreme — and there is no reason for one of these factors to influence the outcome more than the other. Thus, an auspicious sampling situation, which is what a large sample gives us, results in a sampling distribution that represents both ways of being wrong (low side or high side) about equally often, that is, it is symmetric around $\mu_{\overline{X}}$.

In this consideration of normality, it is also clear, and for the same sort of reason, that the sampling distribution will have a tall middle and low tails. If the contemplated sampling is "with replacement," that is, putting each selection back into the pot so that it has a chance of being drawn again, it is possible to draw the same individual 500 times. In our case, that means that the sample mean could be as low as the lowest score on tolerance in the population, or as high as the highest. What, however, is the probability of drawing the same individual 500 times in a row? Obviously, it is very low. If sampling is "without replacement," the sample mean could be as low as the average of the 500 lowest scorers. But in an auspicious sampling situation, such sample values will also be rare. They are possibilities and must therefore be considered as having *some* probability, but their probabilities are very low compared to the probabilities of values that are close to the population mean. All of this is quite simply and directly reflected by the tapering curve of the sampling distribution, which shows the differing probabilities for sample means that are close to and far from the population mean.

The same sort of reasoning applied once more indicates why the sampling distribution has the sort of *dispersion* that it does. Let us say that, by some standard, we considered the distribution of tolerance scores in the population to be wide. Another way of saying the same thing is that we are considering the population standard deviation, σ_X, to be large. Then it follows that, by the same standard, we must consider the *sampling* distribution to be extremely thin by comparison, because it has a standard deviation that is $1/\sqrt{n}$ times the population standard deviation. In our case, the square root of 500 being around 22, the standard deviation of the sampling distribution (not the *sample*, whose standard deviation should be quite similar to that of the population) is only about 1/22 times as large as the standard deviation of the population (see Figures 3.2 and 3.3). That is a huge difference! Why is it so? It is because in an auspicious sampling situation, although extreme values are possible, most of the infinitely many hypothetical sample means will hit pretty close to the population mean; they will deviate only a small amount on either side. That is, the central values are far more probable than the extreme values, so that the average distance off center is very small. We will see that this is a result of great power; it means that, once the real sample is actually drawn and its mean is calculated numerically, if it is off target at all, it is not likely to be off by very much. The probability of being off by a lot is quite low.

The Task

Having established what a sampling distribution is, it remains to detail how it is used in classical inference. Recall that the point of such inference is to learn something about a parameter that we cannot observe, such as a particular population mean, from bits of observed data on a single sample. Learning "something" about the parameter boils down to accomplishing one or both of two tasks.

One task that can be performed relative to the unobserved parameter is to *estimate its magnitude*. It was noted above that a direct estimate based on the sample value would often not be considered good enough. This sort of estimate is called a "point estimate." If our sample mean tolerance is 27.5, for example, then our best point estimate of the unobserved mean tolerance in the population would naturally be 27.5. Another possibility, however, and the one supported by classical inference, is an interval estimate. Here, we would make some estimate on the order of "27.5 ± 3," rather than just 27.5 all by itself. This may seem a peculiar thing to do. Can we really be better off by judging that the mean tolerance score in the population is probably between 24.5 and 30.5, let us say, than by judging that it is probably 27.5? Actually, the answer is yes, we can, in the sense that we have a better chance of being right with the interval estimate because we have allowed ourselves more latitude. But how much better? Perhaps if we knew that, we would have a basis for choosing which estimate to make. Classical inference sup-

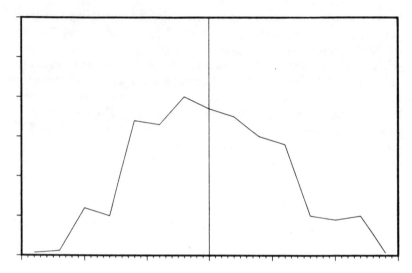

Figure 3.2. Population Distribution

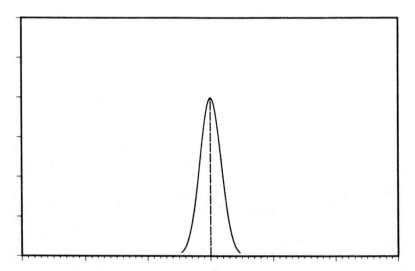

Figure 3.3. Sampling Distribution

plies the answer to that question. It will be the main business of the next section, and in a sense the main business of this monograph, to show just how such a feat is accomplished (as you might guess, the sampling distribution is at the heart of the method). Let it be said here, though, that whereas one may be able to have only very little confidence in the correctness of an estimate such as 27.5 ± .01, it is not at all unusual to be able to reach a conclusion such as 27.5 ± 2, or ± 3, with 95% confidence in the correctness of the estimate, or even more. That classical inference is often able to supply what are still fairly narrow interval estimates with a bare minimum of uncertainty makes it one of the more powerful applied mathematical tools available.

The other sort of task that is often performed relative to the unobserved parameter is to *test specific claims about its magnitude.* Such tests are called tests of significance. The claims might be serious claims advanced by oneself or others, such as a claim that the difference in pay for men and women in comparable jobs is some very large amount, or perhaps some very small one. On the other hand, they might be claims advanced only as straw men, with the hope and expectation of shooting them down. The primary sort of claim in the latter category is a claim that the relationship between two variables is zero. Most tests of significance are of that nature, and the following is the reason why: In social science, researchers are in general engaged in a search for the sorts of factors that make a difference in people's lives, with different aspects of life being salient for different disciplines. To say which factors make a difference is often to say that there is a relationship between such factors and the behaviors or events of concern in the discipline — for example, the factors that make people turn out to vote, or that make them tolerant, or innovative, or apt to be leaders. Thus, if the investigator is able to *reject* the straw-man claim that such a relationship is zero, so that it must be accepted to exist in *some* degree (at least in the group studied), then one has potentially identified such a factor. It is not that simple, of course. For one thing, to have found a relationship is not necessarily to have found a causal relationship. And for another, factors that seem to be important in one population or at one time have an annoying way of appearing to be inconsequential later on. But the identification of such factors at work in at least one setting is a strong beginning for much of the thought and research that must then go on at a deeper level.

Thus, we have indicated two tasks for classical inference in connection with population parameters: interval estimation and significance testing. As noted earlier, we will consider interval estimation first, and then add the twist that is necessary to extend the basic reasoning to significance testing.

4. INTERVAL ESTIMATION

The task, then, is to provide an interval estimate of a population parameter and to know how much confidence to have in its accuracy; our approach to the task will feature the use of a sample statistic together with our knowledge of the relevant sampling distribution. We might as well take a simple statistic for our first illustration: Let us begin by thinking about an interval estimate of a population mean, say the mean tolerance score.

The conceptual procedure for accomplishing the task is best seen as a series of seven steps, some of them a bit tricky. These steps apply, with minor changes, to the case of any parameter and its corresponding statistic, as long as the form of the sampling distribution of the particular statistic is known (a few of the statistics in common use in social science do not have known sampling distributions — the form has not, or at least not yet, been figured out by statisticians). In what follows, you must consider that we know which parameter we want to estimate (e.g., the mean tolerance in a particular population) and we know also that we are going to estimate it by taking a sample of a certain size from the relevant population and calculating the corresponding statistic (the sample mean tolerance). We have not yet, however, drawn the sample. The thinking represented by the seven steps is thinking that we are able to do before the sample is actually observed.

Seven Steps to Interval Estimation for the Population Mean

I will present the seven steps all together first, so that their flow may be comprehended, and then I will elaborate on each. The initial, brief listing will no doubt appear cryptic to the reader, but once the meaning of the steps is fleshed out, so that they communicate adequately even though they are brief, the terseness of this form becomes convenient.

$\bar{X}$1. The $\bar{X}$ I will calculate once I draw my sample is an element located *somewhere* in *some* sampling distribution.

$\bar{X}$2. That sampling distribution of $\bar{X}$ happens to be normal, with mean μ_X and standard deviation $\sigma_X/\sqrt{n}$.

$\bar{X}$3. Select a "worst case" level in percentiles, for example, 5%. In other words, we are working with a confidence level of 95%.

9

$\overline{X}$4. Working with that level, I recognize the following: The probability is .95 that the single $\overline{X}$ I will calculate will be within *some* certain distance of $\mu_{\overline{X}}$. Call that distance the *critical distance.*

$\overline{X}$5. Express the critical distance in terms of number of standard deviations from the mean, as follows: The probability is .95 that the single $\overline{X}$ I will calculate will be within $1.96\sigma_{\overline{X}}$ of $\mu_{\overline{X}}$.

$\overline{X}$6. Express the critical distance in terms of the values of the statistic on the horizontal axis: The probability is .95 that the single $\overline{X}$ I will calculate will be within $1.96(\sigma_X/\sqrt{n})$ of $\mu_{\overline{X}}$.

$\overline{X}$7. Since the probability is .95 that $\overline{X}$ will be within the established critical distance of μ_X, then the probability is .95 that μ_X will be within the established critical distance of $\overline{X}$. This last statement is equivalent to a 95% interval estimate, as follows: With 95% confidence, the interval $\overline{X} \pm 1.96(\sigma_X/\sqrt{n})$ includes μ_X.

Let us expand on the meaning of these seven steps.

$\overline{X}$1. "The $\overline{X}$ I will calculate once I draw my sample is an element located *somewhere* in *some* sampling distribution." Of course this is always true, even if we happen to know nothing about the form and parameters of the particular sampling distribution needed. Note that it makes sense to talk about a sampling distribution even though no sample has yet been drawn; it is the distribution of possibilities.

$\overline{X}$2. "That sampling distribution of $\overline{X}$ happens to be normal, with mean μ_X and standard deviation $\sigma_X/\sqrt{n}$." For the statistic $\overline{X}$, these facts are known on the basis of the Central Limit Theorem. The distribution is depicted in Figure 4.1, which the reader is urged to consult throughout the discussion of these seven steps.

$\overline{X}$3. "Select a 'worst case' level in percentiles, for example, 5%. In other words, we are working with a confidence level of 95%." If the "worst case" selected is 1%, the confidence level is 99%, and so forth. By the term "worst case," I mean the following: Knowing that the $\overline{X}$ I will calculate is located somewhere in some sampling distribution, and that I will use it as a tool for estimating the mean of that sampling distribution, the question of how far away from the mean it is becomes extremely important. We do not know the answer to this, of course, and never will. We can, however, take a worst case, hoping that even that is not so bad. That is, it may be that the sampling distribution is so thin (see Figure 3.3) that even if $\overline{X}$ were about as far away from $\mu_{\overline{X}}$ as it could get, it would still be close enough to be a reasonable estimator. In fact, that is very often the case.

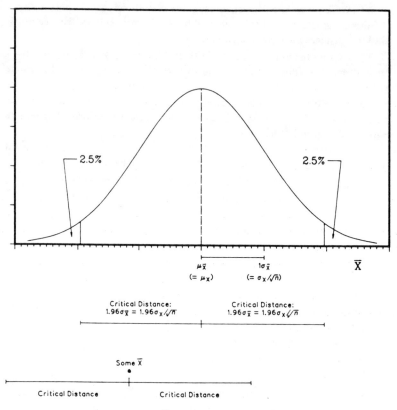

Figure 4.1. The Distribution of $\overline{X}$

Here, then, is the focal point of the method. We are able to do wonderful things with inferential statistics because sampling distributions are often extremely thin distributions. This in turn, remember, results from the fact that, in auspicious sampling, every statistic *tends to be* very representative, that is, very close in magnitude to the corresponding population parameter. We will see that sometimes it does not work out as well as we would like; the sampling distribution for a particular case may be thin, but not really thin enough. When that happens, it is simply too bad. We will have done the best we can, but the best is sometimes not good enough.

Of course (returning to the situation in general, good or bad), we cannot actually afford to take a "worst" case because we must conceive of the sampling distribution as having infinite tails; that is a feature of the mathematical formula that defines a normal distribution. Thus, "worst" will have to mean some location far out in a tail, but not so penalizing as to be infinitely far. We locate the worst-case point in terms of percentiles — always. Considering all of the infinite samples that result from the idea of sampling over and over again forever as being 100% of the cases, we define "worst case" as a location so far out in one of the tails that only, say, $2\frac{1}{2}\%$ of the cases are beyond it (see Figure 4.1). That location would be either the 2.5th percentile (left-hand or negative tail) or the 97.5th percentile (right-hand or positive tail). In either case, 5% of the cases are farther away from the mean, since a case can be farther away in absolute distance by being in either of the two tails. To assume the worst as 5%, therefore, is to assume that the $\overline{X}$ I will calculate is so far out that only 5% of the cases are farther away from the mean. (Remember that 5% of the cases does not mean 5% of the values along the horizontal axis — the first component; it means 5% of all the sample means that would be calculated when sampling forever, some of them coming over and over again — the second component.)

The reader might well ask, "What level or percentile shall I choose as the 'worst'?" The textbook answer is that it depends on how much error you are willing to risk. That is, if you estimate "with 95% confidence," then your procedure, if always followed, would lead you into error 5% of the time. In point of fact, however, social scientists generally do not know how much error they are willing to risk. That is not a very meaningful or relevant concept for us. It is hard to say that there are risks involved as there are, for example, in statistical quality control in industry. If we are truly interested in an interval estimate at all, we are usually trying to get just a rough idea of the magnitude of a parameter, so that if the sampling distribution is thin enough to yield any reasonably narrow interval estimate, that is good enough. Thus, we tend simply to follow convention, and 95% confidence intervals have become conventional. If a 95% interval is too wide to be useful, try 90%. If that still seems too wide, well perhaps this is a case when our best is not quite good enough. We will return below to the factors that make for wider and narrower confidence intervals.

$\overline{X}$4. "Working with that level, I recognize the following: The probability is .95 that the single $\overline{X}$ I will calculate will be within *some* certain distance of $\mu_{\overline{X}}$. Call that distance the *critical distance*." Steps $\overline{X}$4 to $\overline{X}$6 concentrate on measuring the critical distance, that is, the distance between the worst-case point, which is out in a tail, and the mean of the sampling distribution. Step $\overline{X}$4 simply recognizes the existence of such a distance and gives it a name.

$\overline{X}$5. "Express the critical distance in terms of number of standard deviations from the mean, as follows: The probability is .95 that the single $\overline{X}$ I will calculate will be within $1.96\sigma_{\overline{X}}$ of $\mu_{\overline{X}}$." This must seem like a bizarre distraction. Knowing from Step $\overline{X}$4 that the $\overline{X}$ I will calculate is probably not more than a certain distance from $\mu_{\overline{X}}$, I need now to express that distance in terms of points on the tolerance scale. The job of estimating μ_X would be essentially finished now if I could just say that, with .95 probability, the $\overline{X}$ I will calculate will be within three tolerance points of $\mu_{\overline{X}}$, or 2.15 points, or whatever. Why do I not do that? Why begin speaking of standard deviations? The answer is that I do not know (yet) how to associate numbers of points on the tolerance scale with percentiles of the sampling distribution of $\overline{X}$. By simple arithmetic, I can say with .95 probability that $\overline{X}$ will be between the 2.5th and the 97.5th percentile, but how many tolerance points does that represent? How densely are sample mean tolerance scores ranged along the axis of the sampling distribution? Is the distance between the mean of the distribution and the 97.5th percentile a great many tolerance points or just a few? This question, as it happens, is answerable, but not directly; the present step must come between Steps $\overline{X}$4 and $\overline{X}$6.

Two facts make the bridge between Steps $\overline{X}$4 and $\overline{X}$6 possible. One is that in all normal distributions, there is a known and invariable relation between percentiles of the distribution and its standard deviation. The other is that there is a connection between the standard deviation of the sampling distribution of $\overline{X}$ and the standard deviation of the population of scores, such as tolerance scores, on which the sampling distribution is based. We leave the second, which is quite simple, for Step $\overline{X}$6.

It is a property of the normal distribution that a certain distance from the center in terms of standard deviations always represents coverage of the same proportion of the area under the curve, or coverage of the same amount of territory in terms of percentiles. For example, to proceed one standard deviation to the right, starting from the midpoint, is to cover 34.1% of the area under the curve (see Figure 4.2). Since the midpoint is at the 50th percentile, this would place one at the 84.1st percentile. Similarly, proceeding 2.33 standard deviations from the mean covers 49% of the area, bringing one to the 1st or 99th percentile, depending on the direction of travel. Given this property, it is a simple

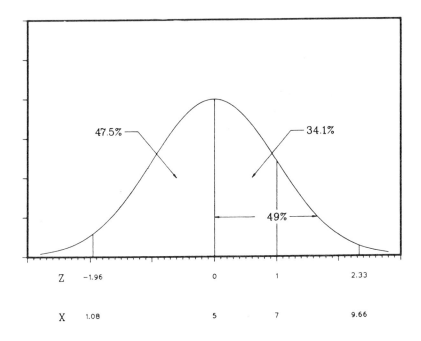

Z: Mean = 0; Standard deviation = 1

X: Mean = 5; Standard deviation = 2

Figure 4.2. Normal and Standard Normal Distributions

matter to express any "worst-case" point in terms of standard deviation units. All one needs is a table giving these invariant relations. *The Z distribution makes such a table convenient,* as we will see in a moment.

What would this table look like? It need not give standard deviation units both above and below the mean because the normal distribution is symmetrical; giving just one-half is adequate. For the half shown, it would merely present standard deviation units, proceeding perhaps by tenths or by hundreths, and associate a percentile or proportion of the area under the curve with each such increment. We would have the number 1 associated with the number 34.1, 2.33 associated with 49, and so on.

Since "1" and "2.33" stand for "1 standard deviation from the mean" and "2.33 standard deviations from the mean," and so forth, it turns out that such a table essentially invents a normal distribution in which the mean is 0 and the standard deviation is equal to 1.0. The reason is the following: For such a distribution, the scores along the axis that are 1 standard deviation above the mean, or 2.33 standard deviations above the mean, would simply be the scores 1 (because in the invented distribution, 1 standard deviation of 1.0 above a mean of 0 would yield a score of 1) or 2.33 (because 2.33 standard deviations of 1.0 above a mean of 0 would equal a score of 2.33), respectively. These are precisely the numbers that would appear in the table we have been discussing. Thus, these numbers do double duty as meaning (1) scores on a normally distributed variable with mean 0 and standard deviation 1.0, and (2) number of standard deviations (of any size) from the mean (no matter what it is) in any normal distribution.

Thus, the table that is generally presented to supply the proportions of area under the curve and number of standard deviations from the mean associated with one another is considered to be a tabular presentation of the normal distribution whose mean is 0 and whose standard deviation is 1.0. That distribution is conventionally called the distribution of the variable, "Z." Since Z is also a surrogate for "number of standard deviations from the mean in a normal distribution," the scores in any normal distribution can be converted to Z scores by expressing them as number of standard deviations from their mean, as follows:

$$Z = \frac{X - \mu_X}{\sigma_X}$$

The numerator of the Z score (or "standard score," as it is often called) gives the distance of a score from the mean of the collectivity, and the denominator serves to express this distance in standard deviation units. For example, if $\mu_X = 5$ and $\sigma_X = 2$, then the Z score corresponding to 7 is 1, and the Z scores corresponding to 9.66 and 1.08 are 2.33 and −1.96, respectively (see Figure 4.2).

Table 4.1 is a table of the Z distribution. It presents exactly the association between proportion of the area under the curve and number of standard deviations from the mean that we have just discussed. $Z = 2.33$ (meaning 2.33 standard deviations above the mean in any normal distribution and, in particular, 2.33 standard deviations of 1.0 above the mean of 0 in *this* distribution) is found by locating the row headed 2.3 and the column headed .03. At the intersection of this row and column is the cell with the entry, 4901, meaning 0.4901 or 49.01% of the area under the curve. $Z = 1.00$ is found by locating the row headed 1.0 and the column headed .00. The cell entry at the intersection is 3413.

TABLE 4.1

Areas under the Normal Curve

Fractional parts of the total area (10,000) under the normal curve, corresponding to distances between the mean and ordinates, which are Z standard-deviation units from the mean.

Z	.00	.01	.02	.03	.04	.05	.06	.07	.08	.09
0.0	0000	0040	0080	0120	0159	0199	0239	0279	0319	0359
0.1	0398	0438	0478	0517	0557	0596	0636	0675	0714	0753
0.2	0793	0832	0871	0910	0948	0987	1026	1064	1103	1141
0.3	1179	1217	1255	1293	1331	1368	1406	1443	1480	1517
0.4	1554	1591	1628	1664	1700	1736	1772	1808	1844	1879
0.5	1915	1950	1985	2019	2054	2088	2123	2157	2190	2224
0.6	2257	2291	2324	2357	2389	2422	2454	2486	2518	2549
0.7	2580	2612	2642	2673	2704	2734	2764	2794	2823	2852
0.8	2881	2910	2939	2967	2995	3023	3051	3078	3106	3133
0.9	3159	3186	3212	3238	3264	3289	3315	3340	3365	3389
1.0	3413	3438	3461	3485	3508	3531	3554	3577	3599	3621
1.1	3643	3665	3686	3718	3729	3749	3770	3790	3810	3830
1.2	3849	3869	3888	3907	3925	3944	3962	3980	3997	4015
1.3	4032	4049	4066	4083	4099	4115	4131	4147	4162	4177
1.4	4192	4207	4222	4236	4251	4265	4279	4292	4306	4319
1.5	4332	4345	4357	4370	4382	4394	4406	4418	4430	4441
1.6	4452	4463	4474	4485	4495	4505	4515	4525	4535	4545
1.7	4554	4564	4573	4582	4591	4599	4608	4616	4625	4633
1.8	4641	4649	4656	4664	4671	4678	4686	4693	4699	4706
1.9	4713	4719	4726	4732	4738	4744	4750	4758	4762	4767
2.0	4773	4778	4783	4788	4793	4798	4803	4808	4812	4817
2.1	4821	4826	4830	4834	4838	4842	4846	4850	4854	4857
2.2	4861	4865	4868	4871	4875	4878	4881	4884	4887	4890
2.3	4893	4896	4898	4901	4904	4906	4909	4911	4913	4916
2.4	4918	4920	4922	4925	4927	4929	4931	4932	4934	4936
2.5	4938	4940	4941	4943	4945	4946	4948	4949	4951	4952
2.6	4953	4955	4956	4957	4959	4960	4961	4962	4963	4964
2.7	4965	4966	4967	4968	4969	4970	4971	4972	4973	4974
2.8	4974	4975	4976	4977	4977	4978	4979	4980	4980	4981
2.9	4981	4982	4983	4984	4984	4984	4985	4985	4986	4986
3.0	4986.5	4987	4987	4988	4988	4988	4989	4989	4989	4990
3.1	4990.0	4991	4991	4991	4992	4992	4992	4992	4993	4993
3.2	4993.129									
3.3	4995.166									
3.4	4996.631									
3.5	4997.674									
3.6	4998.409									
3.7	4998.922									
3.8	4999.277									
3.9	4999.519									
4.0	4999.683									
4.5	4999.966									
5.0	4999.997133									

SOURCE: Rugg (1917:389-390)

What number is associated with a worst-case point of 97.5%? Translating from percentiles to proportion of the area under the curve, we recognize that the 97.5th percentile is at the point such that 47.5% of the area under the curve lies between it and the mean. We work backwards now, from cell entry to column and row headings. Looking for the cell entry closest to 4750, we find that exact number at the intersection of the row headed 1.9 and the column headed .06. Thus, a score at the 97.5th percentile is 1.96 standard deviations of 1.0 above the mean of 0 in the Z distribution, and, in fact, 1.96 standard deviations above the mean in *any* normal distribution. Symmetrically, a score at the 2.5th percentile is 1.96 standard deviations below the mean. Between these two points we have 47.5% plus 47.5%, or 95% of the area (see Figure 4.2).

We see here, then, the origin of our statement in Step $\overline{X}5$: "The probability is .95 that the single $\overline{X}$ I will calculate will be within $1.96\sigma_{\overline{X}}$ of $\mu_{\overline{X}}$." Note that it is not necessary to know what the magnitudes of $\sigma_{\overline{X}}$ and $\mu_{\overline{X}}$ truly are. These symbols merely designate the standard deviation and the mean of the sampling distribution of $\overline{X}$; given that the distribution is normal, the statement is true no matter what these magnitudes may be.

$\overline{X}6$. "Express the critical distance in terms of the values of the statistic on the horizontal axis: The probability is .95 that the single $\overline{X}$ I will calculate will be within $1.96(\sigma_X/\sqrt{n})$ of $\mu_{\overline{X}}$." The statistic on the horizontal axis in our original case is $\overline{X}$, and each point on the axis represents a mean tolerance score for a sample. Having expressed the critical distance in terms of numbers of standard deviations (of the sampling distribution) from the mean in Step $\overline{X}5$, the task is now to convert that metric into the original metric of tolerance scores or, in other research projects, into dollars, voter turnout, points on other attitude scales, and similar, presumably meaningful, measures. This is quite readily and simply accomplished by the knowledge, based on the Central Limit Theorem, that $\sigma_{\overline{X}}$ is equal to $\sigma_X/\sqrt{n}$. (Of course, in real research situations one would essentially never know the magnitude of σ_X, and this is a major problem to be dealt with in the next two sections; for now, let us act as though the quantity were known.) The end result is now in tolerance scores because, it will be remembered, σ_X, or the standard deviation of the tolerance scores in the population, is the "standard" (roughly the average) number of *tolerance points* that each score is away from the mean; it is a statistic expressed in the metric of the original distribution. If n = 500, for example, and if σ_X were, let us say for illustration, 14 points, then $1.96(\sigma_X/\sqrt{n})$ would equal 1.23 points on the tolerance scale. We would know that, with .95 probability, the sample mean we will calculate when we draw the sample of 500 individuals will be within 1.23 points of the population mean tolerance, the value to be estimated.

One is reluctant to be overly dramatic, but it might with some justification be said that we have arrived here at the climax of the tale. We have seen how one sample value plus knowledge of the theoretical sampling distribution enables us to say, at a certain selected level of confidence based on probabilities, that the sample value is within a certain meaningful, interpretable distance of the desired population parameter. We have thus put the unknown parameter squarely and practically within our sights. There is much more to be established, but in a sense it is all elaboration of this basic idea, plus the filling in of some details.

One important caveat is no doubt understood, but should be noted explicitly at this point. To say with 95% confidence that the sample value is within a certain number of tolerance points from the population parameter is also to say that 5% of the time *it will not be within that distance*. Here is the 5% error that results from having to stop somewhere in the infinite tails and say, "this is the worst," when it is truly not; we could possibly draw a sample that is, unknown to us, farther out. Using this exact procedure regularly, we would obtain an interval estimate that did *not* contain the parameter 5% of the time.

$X7$. "Since the probability is .95 that $\bar{X}$ will be within the established critical distance of μ_X, then the probability is .95 that μ_X will be within the established critical distance of $\bar{X}$. This last statement is equivalent to a 95% interval estimate, as follows: with 95% confidence, the interval $\bar{X} \pm 1.96(\sigma_X/\sqrt{n})$ includes μ_X." This step may seem obvious, and we have strongly suggested its content in the previous few paragraphs, but it is an important one to specify anyway, for later purposes. It details how the exact statement of the interval estimate is derived by converting a statement about the distance from sample value to population value into an equivalent statement about the reverse, that is, the distance from population value to sample value. Knowing (with 95% confidence) that the parameter to be estimated is within a certain distance of the sample mean, we merely place that critical distance on either side of the sample mean and infer probabilistically that the parameter is contained in the resulting interval.

Seven Steps, Using the Z Distribution

In this section and the next, we must deal with the problem previously postponed, the problem that we are expressing the critical
distance in terms of an unknown quantity — the standard deviation of
tolerance scores in the population. It is necessary to sneak up on the
solution to this problem, and we do so by beginning with consideration
of interval estimation for μ_X in terms of Z, rather than directly in terms
of $\overline{X}$. The procedure will be to show, by exploiting the Z distribution,
that the central task of interval estimation for μ_X can be accomplished
by means of the sampling distribution of a statistic that is not $\overline{X}$ itself,
but is related to $\overline{X}$ in important ways. That done, we will turn to the t
distribution, which connects both with general interval estimation and
with $\overline{X}$ in the same ways as the Z distribution does, and which also
avoids the need to know the magnitude of σ_X.

The seven steps presented above do not pertain only to the estimation
of μ_X by means of $\overline{X}$. With minor changes, they present a basic pattern
of interval estimation useful in connection with all parameters. In
particular, one might consider estimating the mean of a population of Z
scores. We do not do this because it is a meaningful real-world task — we
already know just by definition that the mean of a population of Z scores
is 0. We do it, rather, because it shows a valuable, indirect method of
estimating μ_X by means of $\overline{X}$. Admittedly, we have already developed a
method — a direct method — just above, but while pedagogically indis-
pensable, that method is ultimately inadequate; it depends on the knowledge of an unknown parameter.

Here are the same seven steps as they would pertain to Z. The reader
is reminded that Z is any normal variable with mean 0 and standard
deviation 1.0; such a variable might be composed and calculated as a
sample statistic in any number of ways, one of which would be

$$Z = \frac{\overline{X} - \mu_{\overline{X}}}{\sigma_{\overline{X}}}$$

Z1. The Z I will calculate once I draw my sample is an element located
somewhere in *some* sampling distribution.

Z2. That sampling distribution of Z happens to be normal, with mean 0 and
standard deviation 1.0 (see Figure 4.3).

Z3. Select a "worst case" level in percentiles, for example, 5%. In other
words, we are working with a confidence level of 95%.

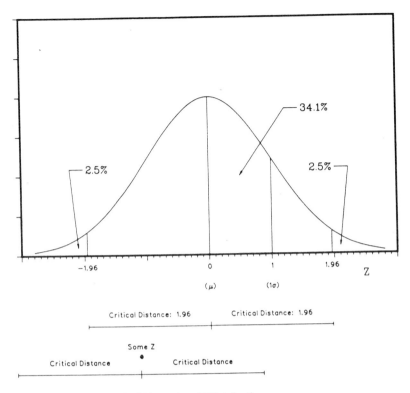

Figure 4.3. The Standard Normal or Z Distribution

Z4. Working with that level, I recognize the following: The probability is .95 that the single Z I will calculate will be within *some* certain distance of 0. Call the distance the *critical distance*.

Z5. (Not necessary, since the standard deviation in this case is simply 1.0.)

Z6. Express the critical distance in terms of the values of the statistic on the horizontal axis: The probability is .95 that the single Z I will calculate will be within 1.96 points of 0.

Z7. Since the probability is .95 that Z will be within the established critical distance of 0, then the probability is .95 that 0 will be within the established critical distance of Z. This last statement is equivalent to a 95% interval estimate, as follows: With 95% confidence, the interval Z ± 1.96 includes 0.

Thus, we have asserted that if we sample and calculate the statistic Z, assuming that our Z is based on a variable that has a normal distribution (such as $\bar{X}$ in the formula above), the probability is .95 that we will obtain some value between -1.96 and $+1.96$. We might not; in fact, we would expect to get a value outside these limits 5% of the time if we constantly used this procedure.

This procedure would seem to be useless, however, because in order to calculate Z in our case, as the above formula clearly shows, one would need not only to know $\sigma_{\bar{X}}$, but $\mu_{\bar{X}}$ as well, and we know neither. We will continue to defer attention to σ_X until later, but $\mu_{\bar{X}}$ may be considered here. It is true that this value is unknown and, in fact, is equal to the mystery parameter that started this whole search. We must therefore give up on the calculation of Z. We may use the seven steps in Z, however, to accomplish exactly what was accomplished in the last section through the first series of seven steps, but in another way. That is, we may use this approach to make the same interval estimate of μ_X on the basis of a sample $\bar{X}$ as before. We begin at step 6 in Z and proceed simply to convert it into step 6 in $\bar{X}$ by means of very simple algebra (to be explained momentarily) as follows:

Z6. $\Pr\{-1.96 < Z < 1.96\} = .95$

Z6A. $\Pr\{-1.96 < [(\bar{X} - \mu_X)/(\sigma_X/\sqrt{n})] < 1.96\} = .95$

Z6B. $\Pr\{-1.96(\sigma_X/\sqrt{n}) < (\bar{X} - \mu_X) < 1.96(\sigma_X/\sqrt{n})] = .95$

$\bar{X}$6. $\Pr\{\mu_X - 1.96(\sigma_X/\sqrt{n}) < \bar{X} < \mu_X + 1.96(\sigma_X/\sqrt{n})\} = .95$

Thus, we end with the precise statement made in step $\bar{X}$6 in the previous section. The algebra is explained as follows: We begin in Z6 with a restatement of step Z6 just above, but in algebraic rather than narrative language. It says simply that, with probability .95, the Z to be calculated from our yet-to-be-drawn sample will be greater than -1.96 and smaller than $+1.96$.

To move to Z6A, simply substitute one way of saying Z for another, as given in the formula for Z above, but with μ_X and $\sigma_X/\sqrt{n}$ replacing their respective equivalents, $\mu_{\bar{X}}$ and $\sigma_{\bar{X}}$.

To move to Z6B, multiply all three sides of the inequality by $\sigma_X/\sqrt{n}$. This is done in order to move toward the isolation of $\bar{X}$, about which we wish to make a statement.

This process is completed in the final step by adding μ_X to all three sides. The resulting statement is an algebraic version of what is stated narratively in Step $\overline{X}6$ of the previous section, namely, that $\overline{X}$ is within the critical distance of μ_X. We are not quite finished, however, because the true aim is to make a statement isolating μ_X, the parameter to be estimated. This is done by starting back at step Z6B and taking the path that isolates μ_X rather than $\overline{X}$:

Z6B. $\Pr\{ -1.96(\sigma_X/\sqrt{n}) < (\overline{X} - \mu_X) < 1.96(\sigma_X/\sqrt{n})\} = .95$
Z6C. $\Pr\{ -\overline{X} - 1.96(\sigma_X/\sqrt{n}) < -\mu_X < -\overline{X} + 1.96(\sigma_X/\sqrt{n})\} = .95$
$\overline{X}7$. $\Pr\{\overline{X} + 1.96(\sigma_X/\sqrt{n}) > \mu_X > \overline{X} - 1.96(\sigma_X/\sqrt{n})\} = .95$
$\overline{X}7A$. $\Pr\{\overline{X} - 1.96(\sigma_X/\sqrt{n}) < \mu_X < \overline{X} + 1.96(\sigma_X/\sqrt{n})\} = .95$

To isolate μ_X in Z6C we have subtracted $\overline{X}$ from all three sides. This does not succeed completely, however, because it leaves us with $-\mu_X$ instead of the positive value. The next step, then, labeled $\overline{X}7$, is to multiply Z6C by -1. That is simple enough, except that when inequalities are concerned rather than ordinary equations (the term "inequalities" refers to statements like equations that use < or > rather than =), the direction of the inequality signs must be reversed when multiplying by a negative number. (The reader can check this quickly by taking an inequality such as $2 < 4 < 6$. To make the resulting statement true when multiplying by -1, we must reverse the directions to yield $-2 > -4 > -6$.) $\overline{X}7A$ is an exact restatement of $\overline{X}7$, but reordering the sides from right to left instead of from left to right. Whereas the previous conclusion, statement $\overline{X}6$, said that $\overline{X}$ is within the selected critical distance of μ_X, the final statement now says that μ_X is within the selected critical distance of $\overline{X}$.

Thus, we have used the estimation logic in conjunction with the sampling distribution of Z to accomplish exactly what was accomplished more directly using $\overline{X}$. This substitution achieves no progress in results toward the goal of estimating μ_X, but it does yield a crucial insight: It is possible to arrive at the estimate using the sampling distribution of a *function* of $\overline{X}$ (namely Z) rather than the sampling distribution of $\overline{X}$ itself. Very simple algebraic manipulations allow us to move from one to the other. This principle does not pertain to $\overline{X}$ and μ_X alone; it is used as well in connection with a large number of totally different parameters.

Seven Steps, Using the *t* Distribution

With the realization that the sampling distribution of a function of $\overline{X}$ may be utilized rather than $\overline{X}$ itself, the thought must naturally occur that other such functions would do just as well as Z, if only their sampling distributions were known. For example, if "G" were some statistic that, unlike $\sigma_X/\sqrt{n}$, could be calculated from the sample to be drawn, and if the sampling distribution of $(\overline{X} - \mu_X)/G$ happened to be known, then we could go through exactly the same algebraic steps as above and obtain the desired interval estimate without confronting the nuisance of the unknown σ_X. What sort of denominator should be used? The most likely thing to try is an estimate of σ_X rather than σ_X itself. Might we simply use the standard deviation of the tolerance scores in the sample to be drawn, s_X, in the denominator in place of σ_X? After all, if the sample is large, then s_X should be quite close in magnitude to σ_X.

In fact, it can be shown that the very best estimator of $\sigma_X/\sqrt{n}$ that we can obtain from a sample is not $s_X/\sqrt{n}$, but $s_X/\sqrt{n-1}$. (The derivation of this fact need not concern us here, but the interested reader might consult Hays, 1981:187-189.) There is a problem, however, in using this statistic in the denominator in place of $\sigma_X/\sqrt{n}$: Technically speaking, the result no longer has the Z distribution. That means that the Z table is no longer any good to us for associating the value we would calculate, $s_X/\sqrt{n-1}$, with proportions of area under the curve in a sampling distribution. Whereas before we had a known sampling distribution but were unable to calculate the relevant statistic, we now have a statistic we can calculate completely but have lost our connection with the known sampling distribution. The solution to the problem is to recognize that $(\overline{X} - \mu_X)/(s_X/\sqrt{n-1})$ also has a sampling distribution of some sort and, if possible, to figure out what it is; if not, we must try for another denominator, or perhaps another function of $\overline{X}$ and μ_X altogether.

The task of figuring out the sampling distribution of $(\overline{X} - \mu_X)/(s_X/\sqrt{n-1})$ was accomplished by W. S. Gosset in 1908. Since Gosset wrote under the pen name "Student" and called his distribution the *t* distribution, it is often known as Student's *t* distribution. It is not only $(\overline{X} - \mu_X)/(s_X/\sqrt{n-1})$ that has this particular sampling distribution; a large number of other commonly needed statistics have it as well, so that the achievement was indeed a major one.

The *t* distribution looks very much like the Z distribution; it is bell-shaped and symmetrical around a mean of 0. The main difference is that it has relatively more cases or area in the tails and relatively less area in the interior. In spite of the similarity in looks, it may be noted in passing that the formula for this frequency distribution is totally different from that of the normal distribution.

To say that the distribution of the statistic t is known is to say "If you give me the value of any t that you might calculate from a sample, I can tell you where, in terms of percentiles, that value is located in the sampling distribution." We have a table that makes these associations. Thus, if $(\bar{X} - \mu_X)/(s_X/\sqrt{n-1})$ has the t distribution, we let a particular $(\bar{X} - \mu_X)/(s_X/\sqrt{n-1})$ equal t and look up the percentile value for that number in the t table. If we knew that another, totally different statistic also was distributed as t, we could set a calculated value of that statistic equal to t and pursue the same process.

There is just one further complication to observe before we can accomplish the original task, it now being evident that we actually will be able to achieve the goal. The complication is that there is not just one t distribution, but many. The formula has a parameter in it called "the degrees of freedom," so that for every different value taken by the degrees of freedom, the whole table of associations is different. It is not enough, therefore, to say that a particular statistic has the t distribution; it is necessary to know that it has the t distribution with so many degrees of freedom. In our case, $(\bar{X} - \mu_X)/(s_X/\sqrt{n-1})$, it is known that this statistic has the t distribution with $n - 1$ degrees of freedom, or, in other words, the degrees of freedom are equal to one less than the sample size. When we calculate the value of t, therefore, we need to refer it to a table of t with $n - 1$ degrees of freedom to obtain the proper association between values of t and proportions of area under the curve. This would seem to involve the onerous necessity of printing a very large number of t tables in the backs of statistics books, but the problem is circumvented by printing only the most commonly used parts of such tables. That way, each "table" takes only one line, and all of them that one would ever need can be put onto one page. We will consult that page in a moment. First, let us see that we may accomplish our major task in the same pattern as before. For the sake of clarity in learning how to get about in the t tables, we will make just one change in the sampling situation we have in mind; let us now assume that our sample size is only 26 instead of 500.

The same seven steps proceed as follows:

*t*1. The *t* I will calculate once I draw my sample is an element located *somewhere* in *some* sampling distribution.

*t*2. That sampling distribution happens to be known; call it the "*t* distribution with 25 degrees of freedom." It has a mean of 0 (see Figure 4.4).

*t*3. Select a "worse-case" level in percentiles, for example, 5%. In other words, we will work with a confidence level of 95%.

*t*4. Working with that level, I recognize the following: The probability is .95 that the single *t* I will calculate will be within *some* certain distance of 0. Call that distance the *critical distance*.

*t*5. (Not relevant; standard-deviation units are not associated with percentiles in the *t* distribution as they are in the normal distribution.)

*t*6. Express the critical distance in terms of the value of the statistic on the horizontal axis: The probability is .95 that the single *t* I will calculate will be within 2.06 points of 0.

*t*7. Since the probability is .95 that *t* will be within the established critical distance of 0, then the probability is .95 that 0 will be within the established critical distance of *t*. This last statement is equivalent to a 95% interval estimate, as follows: With 95% confidence, the interval *t* ± 2.06 includes 0.

It is clear that this series of steps is almost identical with the series in Z except that in steps 6 and 7 we find the value 2.06 instead of 1.96, as before. Turning to Table 4.2, we find that the left-hand column is headed "df," for degrees of freedom. Looking down that column for 25, which is one less than our illustrative sample size, and then looking across for the column headed .05 for a two-tailed test (to be explained below), we see the cell value of 2.06: that is, for 25 degrees of freedom, $t = 2.06$ is at the point where 2.5% of the cases are beyond that *t* value in each tail. Glancing down to the bottom of the table, we also see that if our illustrative sample size had been 500 again, the value of *t* associated with 5% of the cases would have been 1.96, just as it is in the Z distribution: for large samples, the *t* distribution tends toward the exact shape of the Z distribution. As before, however, the conclusion in step *t*7 is not of value in itself, but only as it will enable a conversion into a statement about $\overline{X}$ and μ_X instead of *t*. The algebra to accomplish this is identical with the algebra for converting from Z to $\overline{X}$, as follows:

*t*6. $\Pr\{-2.06 < t < 2.06\} = .95$

*t*6A. $\Pr\{-2.06 < [(\overline{X} - \mu_X)/(s_X/\sqrt{n-1})] < 2.06\} = .95$

*t*6B. $\Pr\{-2.06(s_X/\sqrt{n-1}) < (\overline{X} - \mu_X) < 2.06(s_X/\sqrt{n-1})\} = .95$

*t*6C. ($cf.\overline{X}6$). $\Pr\{\mu_X - 2.06(s_X/\sqrt{n}-1) < \overline{X} < \mu_X + 2.06(s_X/\sqrt{n-1})\} = .95$

45

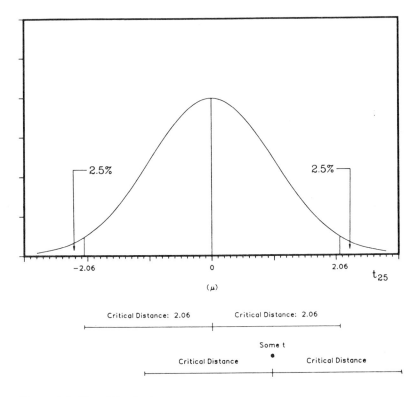

Figure 4.4. The *t* Distribution

Here, we arrive at a statement isolating $\overline{X}$ exactly as before, except that we started with the appropriate statement about t, rather than Z, and substituted accordingly in t6A. Having done so, the working expression is free of σ_X. To move to the statement that isolates μ_X, we back up just as previously and finally arrive at the destination:

t6B. $\Pr\{-2.06(s_X/\sqrt{n-1}) < (\overline{X} - \mu_X) < 2.06(s_X/\sqrt{n-1})\} = .95$
t6B1. $\Pr\{-\overline{X} - 2.06(s_X/\sqrt{n-1}) < -\mu_X < -\overline{X} + 2.06(s_X/\sqrt{n-1})\} = .95$
t6D. (*cf.*X7). $\Pr\{\overline{X} + 2.06(s_X/\sqrt{n-1}) > \mu_X > \overline{X} - 2.06(s_X/\sqrt{n-1})\} = .95$
t6D1. (*cf.*$\overline{X}$7A). $\Pr\{\overline{X} - 2.06(s_X/\sqrt{n-1}) < \mu_X < \overline{X} + 2.06(s_X/\sqrt{n-1})\} = .95$

Recall that before we assumed for illustrative purposes that the unknown parameter σ_X was equal to 14 tolerance points. Here we do

46

TABLE 4.2
Distribution of *t*

df	Level of significance for one-tailed test					
	.10	.05	.025	.01	.005	.0005
	Level of significance for two-tailed test					
	.20	.10	.05	.02	.01	.001
1	3.078	6.314	12.706	31.821	63.657	636.619
2	1.886	2.920	4.303	6.965	9.925	31.598
3	1.638	2.353	3.182	4.541	5.841	12.941
4	1.533	2.132	2.776	3.747	4.604	8.610
5	1.476	2.015	2.571	3.365	4.032	6.859
6	1.440	1.943	2.447	3.143	3.707	5.959
7	1.415	1.895	2.365	2.998	3.499	5.405
8	1.397	1.860	2.306	2.896	3.355	5.041
9	1.383	1.833	2.262	2.821	3.250	4.781
10	1.372	1.812	2.228	2.764	3.169	4.587
11	1.363	1.796	2.201	2.718	3.106	4.437
12	1.356	1.782	2.179	2.681	3.055	4.318
13	1.350	1.771	2.160	2.650	3.012	4.221
14	1.345	1.761	2.145	2.624	2.977	4.140
15	1.341	1.753	2.131	2.602	2.947	4.073
16	1.337	1.746	2.120	2.583	2.921	4.015
17	1.333	1.740	2.110	2.567	2.898	3.965
18	1.330	1.734	2.101	2.552	2.878	3.922
19	1.328	1.729	2.093	2.539	2.861	3.883
20	1.325	1.725	2.086	2.528	2.845	3.850
21	1.323	1.721	2.080	2.518	2.831	3.819
22	1.321	1.717	2.074	2.508	2.819	3.792
23	1.319	1.714	2.069	2.500	2.807	3.767
24	1.318	1.711	2.064	2.492	2.797	3.745
25	1.316	1.708	2.060	2.485	2.787	3.725
26	1.315	1.706	2.056	2.479	2.779	3.707
27	1.314	1.703	2.052	2.473	2.771	3.690
28	1.313	1.701	2.048	2.467	2.763	3.674
29	1.311	1.699	2.045	2.462	2.756	3.659
30	1.310	1.697	2.042	2.457	2.750	3.646
40	1.303	1.684	2.021	2.423	2.704	3.551
60	1.296	1.671	2.000	2.390	2.660	3.460
120	1.289	1.658	1.980	2.358	2.617	3.373
∞	1.282	1.645	1.960	2.326	2.576	3.291

SOURCE: Table 4.2 is abridged from Table III of Fisher and Yates (1948). Used by permission.

not have to make such assumptions. Statement t6D1 is a statement that can be made before any sampling is carried out, but now the time has come to draw the sample and, just as we will calculate $\overline{X}$, we will also calculate s_X, that is, we need both the mean and the standard deviation of the tolerance scores in the sample we draw in order to make our actual calculations. Let us suppose for illustration that the sample mean turned out to be 60 and the sample standard deviation 14.

We would then estimate that the unknown population mean tolerance score lies in the interval $60 \pm 2.06(14/\sqrt{25})$, or 60 ± 5.77. That is, we may say with 95% confidence that the population mean lies in the interval between 54.23 and 65.77.

Conclusion

Several observations should be made before transferring what has been learned about interval estimation to the question of tests of significance.

First, it is plain that we were able to accomplish what we did by having at our disposal the known sampling distribution of a statistic — in this case, $(\overline{X} - \mu_X)/(s_X/\sqrt{n-1})$ — that is a function of both the parameter (μ_X) and the statistic $(\overline{X})$ at issue. That seems plain enough, in fact, quite straightforward. It is a serious mistake, however, to think on the basis of that recognition that the idea of interval estimation is easy to comprehend. The apparent simplicity of the final step is deceptive. If in fact one were to ask the ordinary veteran scientist to explain the basis for an interval estimate, it is likely that it would take him or her hours or days of thought to be able to do so, and then only with pencil and paper in hand. Do not forget what we went through to arrive at the end point. One needs to know what a sampling distribution is and have that firmly in mind. Given that, one may indeed say, "I know that there is a statistic, $(\overline{X} - \mu_X)/(s_X/\sqrt{n-1})$, that has the t distribution with $n-1$ degrees of freedom, and from that I can derive the interval estimate required," but that sort of statement is strange, sudden, disembodied. How and why did anyone ever get to that? It seems to have no apparent rationale. It is a good place to begin an explanation, perhaps, once the basics have been learned, but then one has to back up to remember where it came from. Otherwise, one is dealing only in "cookbook statistics" — simply applying formulas to apparently relevant cases by virtue of rote learning. One needs to know about the form and parameters of the sampling distribution of the mean itself, the abstract relation between sample means and percentiles of that sampling distribution, the relation between standard deviation units and percentiles in that distribution, the crucial function of a worst-case assumption, the ability to convert from standard deviation units to the metric sought, the problem that the metric sought contains an unknown quantity, the relation between the distributions of Z and $\overline{X}$, and the insight that estimates may be made on the basis of functions of a statistic as well as the statistic itself. In short, the beginning student should not jump to the conclusion that the material has been mastered when the final step is understood, and should also not despair if it appears difficult to keep all of the background procedures and methods in mind. Most of us never can keep them in mind; we have to think the process through again and again.

Second, many readers no doubt observed with some consternation that the interval we ended up with in this illustration was a wide one: The mean tolerance score in the population, we may say with 95% confidence, is in the interval 60 ± 5.77, or 54.23 to 65.77. Perhaps that is good enough for one's particular purpose, but it is certainly possible that such a wide estimate is not good enough; we might need an estimate more on the order of sample mean plus or minus 2.5 points, let us say, or even 2 points. What determines how wide the interval estimate is, and what can be done to make it narrower and therefore probably more useful? A glance at the algebraic expression for the critical distance, $2.06(14/\sqrt{25})$, or, in abstract terms, $t_{n-1;.025} (s_X/\sqrt{n-1})$, makes it clear that three elements govern the width of the interval: the level selected for the worst-case t, the standard deviation of tolerance scores in the sample, and the sample size. Let us examine the importance of each of these in turn.

1. *The worst-case level.* It is clear from the t tables that if we had chosen a worst-case level closer to the center instead of so far out in the tails, the interval would have been smaller. For example, if we had chosen the 10% level instead of the 5% level, we would have been able to multiply by 1.708 instead of 2.06. It is just as clear, however, that in that case we would have been only 90% confident of our estimate instead of 95%. That is, step t6 would have read in part: "The probability is .90 that the single t I will calculate will be within 1.708 points of 0." There is therefore an inescapable trade-off. By tinkering just a little bit with the worst-case level selected, one may obtain either a relatively wide interval estimate in which one has a great deal of confidence, or a relatively narrow one in which one has only moderate confidence. As indicated earlier, the issue is one to be decided by the needs or feelings of the investigator in the individual case.

2. *The sample standard deviation.* Given the formula for the critical distance, the larger the sample standard deviation, the larger the interval estimate. The factor that governs the size of s_X is the standard deviation of tolerance scores in the population, σ_X. The first is a reflection of the second by virtue of deriving from a random sample. Of course, the investigator has no control over σ_X; it is what it is. We profit only by understanding that relatively narrow interval estimates must be considered difficult to achieve when the population standard deviation is, to the best of our knowledge, quite large.

3. *The sample size.* Being the denominator in the formula for the critical distance, it is clear that the larger the sample, the narrower the estimate. Recall how narrow our illustrative interval estimate was when we were thinking in terms of a sample of 500. Instead of 60 ± 5.77, as here, a sample size of 501, using the *t* distribution, would yield 60 ± 1.23, a very narrow and almost undoubtedly useful interval estimate indeed. This effect of sample size is intuitively reasonable because large samples yield very thin sampling distributions — almost every single large-sample mean in the infinite collection will be very accurately reflective of the population mean itself. Thus, if accuracy is important, a large sample is advised. The only sort of thing that stands in the way of using very large samples all of the time is expense.

Finally, it is desirable to note what might be considered a technicality about the sort of statement we make in presenting a statistical confidence interval. Although a technicality, it is worth reviewing for the sake of conceptual clarity. It is necessary to see that the statement, "The probability is .95 that the interval $\overline{X} \pm k$ includes μ_X," is not a statement about μ_X; μ_X is either in that interval or not; that is, it is in there either with probability 1.0 or with probability 0, and not anything in between. The magnitude of μ_X is a real, empirical fact, something that already exists. The classical statistican would no more attach probabilities to it than he or she would say that the probability is .4 that it rained yesterday. Instead, the statement in quotes is a statement about the *interval*: The probability is indeed .95 that this interval includes μ_X, since 95% of the time I will select a sample whose mean tolerance score is in the interior of the sampling distribution rather than in one of the 2.5% tails.

5. SIGNIFICANCE TESTING

I proposed earlier that one might entertain two tasks for classical inference in connection with an unobserved population parameter. One is to estimate what the magnitude of that parameter is. The previous section on Interval Estimation was concerned with that particular task. The second was to test specific claims about the parameter's magnitude. That process is called "hypothesis testing," or "significance testing." One might want at times to test a claim about a univariate parameter such as a population mean or variance. The great bulk of such tests by far, however, concern bivariate or multivariate parameters, that is, parameters that indicate relationships. Furthermore, most such claims are straw-man claims. We are interested in establishing that a certain relationship exists. If we can use statistics to *reject*, with substantial confidence, the straw-man claim that the relationship is zero, then we have discovered just the sort of thing we suspected and wanted to confirm. In that way, the straw-man claim becomes a very important logical device. To speak most usefully about significance tests, therefore, it will be well to frame the discussion in terms of statistics that indicate a relationship.

Two fundamental and simple bivariate statistics are the difference-of-means and the difference-of-proportions. To use the difference-of-proportions, both variables in question must be dichotomous, or two-valued. If tolerance were our result or outcome variable, for example, people might be scored somehow as either "tolerant" or "intolerant." Let us say that ambition was our presumed causal variable (although we will not yet deal with the question of demonstrating causality, only of relationship). Individuals might then somehow be scored also as either "ambitious" or "not ambitious." Thus, each individual has a score on two variables, ambition and tolerance. We might have the idea and therefore the research prediction that ambition (among other factors) determines tolerance in a given population. We would therefore suppose that ambition and tolerance are related in that population in such a way either that (1) ambitious people tend to be intolerant and unambitious people tolerant (negative relationship — the more ambitious, the less tolerant), or (2) the ambitious people tend to be the more tolerant (positive relationship). In either case, or even if we did not want to predict which category tended to be more tolerant, we could test the straw-man hypothesis, called the "null" hypothesis, that the relationship between ambition and tolerance is zero, with the research prediction that this hypothesis will in fact be rejected.

Having a measurement scale that assigns tolerance scores between zero and one hundred, we might want to take advantage of this finer discrimination rather than simply categorizing people as tolerant or intolerant. The finer scale encourages the calculation of mean tolerance scores. Ambition still being a dichotomy, we might then test a straw-man null hypothesis about a difference-of-means, that is, the null hypothesis that the average tolerance score among ambitious people in the population is just the same as the average tolerance score among the unambitious.

In either case — difference-of-means or difference-of-proportions — note that the parameter is still only one number, albeit a more complicated one than in the case of the simple mean, as considered in prior sections. If we symbolize tolerance by Y, as is common for effect or outcome variables, then the difference-of-means might by symbolized as $(\mu_{Y2} - \mu_{Y1})$. If, say, the mean tolerance score among ambitious people in the population (group 2) was 45, and among the unambitious (group 1) it was 59, then the difference-of-means would be 45 – 59, or −14, one number still, but a number that is a bit more elaborate to calculate than a simple mean.

Let us continue to think in terms of the difference-of-means; almost everything we do will hold as a basic pattern for the difference-of-proportions, and in fact for all other bivariate statistics as well. The one number we use to express the relationship would have been arrived at by a different route and the relevant sampling distribution might be different, but the fundamental logic of the test is always the same.

The task, then, is to test the straw-man claim that the difference-of-means in the population, $(\mu_{Y2} - \mu_{Y1})$, is zero. Our vehicle will naturally be to draw a sample, split it into two subgroups by means of our measurement of ambition, and calculate the mean tolerance score in each subgroup. Then we can subtract one subsample mean from the other. The resulting difference-of-means in the sample might well be symbolized as $(\bar{Y}_2 - \bar{Y}_1)$, again one number. This sample difference might be −14, or −5, or 8, and so forth. In any case, we would use that sample value to make an inference about the population difference-of-means, that is, to infer whether or not $(\mu_{Y2} - \mu_{Y1})$ is zero.

The Indirect or Interval-Estimation Method

We already know one excellent method of accomplishing this. We may construct an interval estimate in exactly the way set out in the previous section, but using $(\mu_{Y2} - \mu_{Y1})$ and $(\bar{Y}_2 - \bar{Y}_1)$ in the place of μ_X and $\bar{X}$. *The test would consist simply in ascertaining whether the interval estimate, arrived at in the normal way, includes zero.* Our confidence interval conclusion would have the form: I can say with 95% confidence that $(\mu_{Y2} - \mu_{Y1})$ is in the interval $(\overline{Y}_2 - \overline{Y}_1) \pm$ some particular number (the critical distance). Putting that critical distance on either side of the observed sample value, the single number $(\overline{Y}_2 - \overline{Y}_1)$, I would then see if the resulting numerical interval includes zero or not. The interval estimate –3 to 9, for example, includes zero, whereas the interval estimate –11 to –3 does not. If the interval does not include zero, my interval estimate of $(\mu_{Y2} - \mu_{Y1})$ enables me to reject the claim that $(\mu_{Y2} - \mu_{Y1})$ is equal to zero with 95% confidence. The more conventional teminology would have us say that we can reject the claim that $(\mu_{Y2} - \mu_{Y1})$ is equal to zero at the 5% level of significance, that is, with only 5% chance of error.

All that is necessary to pursue this method is the known sampling distribution of the statistic "difference-of-means" plus a knowledge of where in that distribution the population parameter, $(\mu_{Y2} - \mu_{Y1})$, is located. Is the parameter located at the center of the sampling distribution, as was the case with μ_X and $\overline{X}$? Or, we might use a composite sort of statistic by which we can arrive at the goal using the algebraic steps of the previous section. In fact, for large samples the sampling distribution of $(\overline{Y}_2 - \overline{Y}_1)$ is normal, with mean $(\mu_{Y2} - \mu_{Y1})$ and standard deviation

$$\sqrt{(\sigma_1^2/n_1) + (\sigma_2^2/n_2)}.$$

(The symbols under the radical sign are translated as the variance of tolerance scores in subgroup 1, unambitious, divided by the number of unambitious people in the sample, plus the variance of tolerance scores in subgroup 2 divided by the number of ambitious people in the sample. The subscript Y indicating tolerance scores is simply omitted for convenience and considered understood.)

Clearly, however, we have the same difficulty here as before, namely, that the interval cannot be constructed without knowing the variance of tolerance scores among the ambitious and unambitious subgroups in the population. Fortunately, it turns out that the following statistic has the t distribution with $n_1 + n_2 - 2$ degrees of freedom:

$$t = \frac{(\overline{Y}_2 - \overline{Y}_1) - (\mu_{Y2} - \mu_{Y1})}{\sqrt{[s_1^2/(n_1 - 1)] + [s_2^2/(n_2 - 1)]}}$$

This statistic can be calculated using only sample data and isolating the one unknown quantity, $(\mu_{Y2} - \mu_{Y1})$, the quantity we want to estimate as a basis of the test of significance. Let us say, for example, that the mean tolerance score among the ambitious people in the sample turns out to be 45 and among the unambitious, 59. *Note that by this fact we see that there is a relationship, whose magnitude happens to be –14, between ambition and tolerance in the sample; we need no tests or estimates to arrive at this fact of observation.* Let us say as well that the variance of tolerance scores among the ambitious people in the sample was 196 and among the unambitious, 169, while the respective subsample sizes for the ambitious and unambitious were 58 and 64. Starting out with the above statistic having the t distribution with $n_1 + n_2 - 2$ degrees of freedom, and referring this to the algebraic steps involving the t distribution in the previous section, we would have the following statement, exactly comparable to $t6D1$:

$$\Pr\left\{(\overline{Y}_2 - \overline{Y}_1) - 1.98\sqrt{[s_1^2/(n_1 - 1)] + [s_2^2/(n_2 - 1)]} < (\mu_{Y2} - \mu_{Y1})\right.$$
$$\left. < (\overline{Y}_2 - \overline{Y}_1) + 1.98\sqrt{[s_1^2/(n_1 - 1)] + [s_2^2/(n_2 - 1)]} \right\} = .95$$

The number 1.98 comes from the t table for $n_1 + n_2 - 2$ or in this case $58 + 64 - 2 = 120$ degrees of freedom. Filling in the rest of the illustrative data just given, we have the estimate

$$\Pr\left\{(45 - 59) - 1.98\sqrt{169/63 + 196/57} < (\mu_{Y2} - \mu_{Y1})\right.$$
$$\left. < (45 - 59) + 1.98\sqrt{169/63 + 196/57} \right\} = .95$$

$$\Pr\left\{-14 - (1.98)(2.47) < (\mu_{Y2} - \mu_{Y1}) < -14 + (1.98)(2.47)\right\} = .95$$

$$\Pr\left\{-14 - 4.89 < (\mu_{Y2} - \mu_{Y1}) < -14 + 4.89\right\} = .95$$

In other words, we have the estimate that the parameter $(\mu_{Y2} - \mu_{Y1})$ — the difference in mean tolerance scores between ambitious and unambitious people in the population — is in the interval -14 ± 4.89, with 95% confidence. Clearly, this interval estimate of the population parameter, which runs from -18.89 to -9.11, does not include zero. By this indirect route, therefore, we may reject the hypothesis that $(\mu_{Y2} - \mu_{Y1}) = 0$ at the 5% level of significance. We reject the straw-man claim that there is no relationship between ambition and tolerance in the population; on the contrary, it appears from the sample data and the interval estimate that there probably is a relationship, and in fact a negative one, such that the unambitious are more tolerant than the ambitious.

In effect, then, the statement, "My sample result is significant at the 5% level," which is the sort of statement we will want to make in testing claims about relationships, can always be interpreted as meaning: "I put a 95% confidence interval around my sample relationship and it did not include zero." However, the interval-estimate logic is a bit elaborate to wade through and clumsy for some purposes. In particular it would be quite cumbersome to approach the very important procedure of one-tailed testing with the interval-estimate logic as the basis, as well as the concept of Type II errors, and these are both ideas that we will want to develop. Therefore, we will trace another but of course closely related logic in the next section.

The Direct Method of Significance Testing

Intuitively, the idea involved in the ordinary, direct significance test is quite simple. If a sample is a random sample from a certain population, then it ought to resemble that population pretty closely. Or, to say exactly the same thing the other way around, the population ought to resemble the sample. Consider an observed sample difference-of-means, say −14. If a claim about the population from which the sample was drawn is that the corresponding difference-of-means is some number very close to −14, it is believable that our observed sample could indeed have been drawn at random from a population with such a parameter, and there is no apparent basis for rejecting that particular claim about the population. The resemblance is strong. However, if the claimed population difference-of-means is some number that is very far from −14, then the truth of the claim would make our sample a very unrepresentative one. Since our sample is a random sample from the population in question, believing the claim would imply that our sample is an improbable one — possible, perhaps, but improbable. Why, in that case, would anyone believe the claim? The *sample* value, after all, is *real*; the population value is just somebody's guess. On this basis, *rejecting* the claim becomes a reasonable, and in fact the most reasonable, option. In short, we reject claims about population parameters if they are just too far away from the relevant observed sample statistic to make them believable.

The question, of course, is, "How far is too far? Just how far away is so far as to imply a highly improbable sample?" But this is an easy question to answer now. The answer is: "beyond the critical distance."

Furthermore we have all the tools and concepts needed to establish what that distance is and to understand how it functions.

Consider the straw-man claim that the population difference-of-means is 0. Can I reject that claim or not? Let me draw a sample from the population and see how close the resemblance is. Assume that the sample difference-of-means is −14. We know from the interval-estimation method that this value is *beyond the critical distance* away from 0; we know it because we put the critical distance on either side of −14 and 0 was not included in the resulting interval. Therefore, it seems, we should reject the hypothesis of 0. How can we understand this more directly, without recourse to the interval?

The answer is this: First, *assume* that the population from which we are about to draw our sample has, as in the straw-man claim, a difference of mean tolerance scores of zero between the ambitious and the unambitious subgroups. Zero, then, becomes the mean of our hypothetical sampling distribution of the difference-of-means. Here is a crucial step. We assume that the straw-man or other claim is true so that we can see how a real sample looks in comparison with this null hypothesis.

Second, decide on a definition of "improbable" for this case. For example, let us say that if the sample difference-of-means is so far from zero in the sampling distribution that a value so distant would occur less than 5% of the time under the above assumption about the population, then it is an improbable sample under that assumption. How do we decide on 5% rather that 10% or 1%, and so on? We will see that, as before, the decision should reflect the chance of error we are willing to risk in rejecting the straw-man claim when it is in fact true.

Third, establish the decision rule that if, and only if, the sample difference-of-means falls beyond the critical value corresponding to 5% probability, therefore appearing to be a highly improbable sample, then the null hypothesis is to be rejected (see Figure 5.1). After all, the sample value is real and the population value is only a claim.

Lastly, notice that one may sometimes fall into error in making such a rejection — the error of rejecting the null hypothesis when it is in fact true. This is called a "Type I" error. I have, in fact, a 5% likelihood of making a Type I error because, if the straw-man claim about the population is true, 5% of all sample differences-of-means will indeed have values more distant from zero than the critical value. Thus, the critical distance that I established translates into a probability of falling into error by rejecting the null hypothesis when it is true. Knowing this,

56

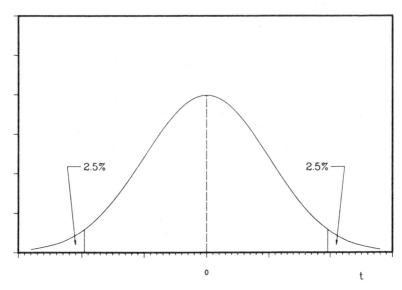

Figure 5.1. A Two-Tailed *t* Test

I should establish the critical distance on that basis, that is, set it at the 5% point if I am willing to risk 5% chance of error, and so forth.

All that now remains is to figure out what the critical value must be in research measurement terms (e.g., tolerance score terms) rather than probability terms. That is, we must answer the question, "What value is it such that sample differences-of-means farther than that distance from zero will occur less than 5% of the time, assuming that the population parameter is indeed zero?" Unfortunately, it is not possible to answer that question without knowing the population subsample variances. It is possible, however, to discover a proper critical value for the sample difference-of-means using the *t* distribution and a bit of algebra exactly comparable to the algebra we used before.

Before launching into that procedure, however, note that in resorting to the *t* distribution we abandon the nice, clean, clear sampling distribution of the difference-of-means. It is not practically useful to us because it has unknown parameters. Thus, we cannot determine *the* sample difference-of-means so distant that it and values farther out occur less than 5% of the time when sampling from this population. Instead, in using *t*, we must settle for a certain combination of a sample difference-of-means, subsample variances, and subsample sizes that is so distant that it and comparably calculated values farther out occur less than 5% of the time. Or, in other words, we settle for a sample difference-of-means so distant that it and values farther out occur less than 5% of the time when sampling from this population, *given* the subsample variances and sizes that we obtain in our actual sample, or *when* the subsample variances and sizes are what they actually turned out to be.

To proceed then, we know that the relevant statistic has as its sampling distribution the t distribution with $n_1 + n_2 - 2$ degrees of freedom, as follows:

$$t = \frac{(\overline{Y}_2 - \overline{Y}_1) - (\mu_{Y2} - \mu_{Y1})}{\sqrt{[s_1^2/(n_1 - 1)] + [s_2^2/(n_2 - 1)]}}$$

Knowing the t distribution with $n_1 + n_2 - 2 = 120$ degrees of freedom, we know that values of t near zero have high relative frequencies, whereas values of t out in the tails have low ones. In particular, we see from table 4.2 that the value -1.98 is at the 2.5th percentile and 1.98 is at the 97.5th. Thus, we know what critical value to use in terms of t. Now, we need only to convert this to tolerance-score terms. Starting from there and using the illustrative data from above, *plus the assumption that the population difference-of-means is zero,* we find the critical value for $(\overline{Y}_2 - \overline{Y}_1)$ as follows:

$\Pr\{t < -1.98 \text{ or} > 1.98\} = .05$

$\Pr\{[(\overline{Y}_2 - \overline{Y}_1) - (\mu_{Y2} - \mu_{Y2})]/\sqrt{[s_1^2/(n_1 - 1)] + [s_2^2/(n_2 - 1)]}$

$\qquad < -1.98 \text{ or} > 1.98\} = .05$

$\Pr\{(\overline{Y}_2 - \overline{Y}_1) - (\mu_{Y2} - \mu_{Y1}) < -1.98\sqrt{[s_1^2/(n_1 - 1)] + [s_2^2/(n_2 - 1)]} \text{ or} >$

$\qquad\qquad 1.98\sqrt{[s_1^2/(n_1 - 1)] + [s_2^2/(n_2 - 1)]} \} = .05$

$\Pr\{(\overline{Y}_2 - \overline{Y}_1) - 0 < (-1.98)(2.47) \text{ or} > (1.98)(2.47)\} = .05$

$\Pr\{(\overline{Y}_2 - \overline{Y}_1) < -4.89 \text{ or} > 4.89\} = .05$

Thus, by starting with a critical value for t, we see that the critical value for the sample difference-of-means in our case (that is, given our subsample sizes and variances) is ±4.89. This, of course, is what we earlier labeled the "critical distance," and we are in fact utilizing it in exactly the same way. The critical distance for t (at the 95% level) is simply the distance that, starting from the midpoint, covers 47.5% of the area under the curve, or 47.5% of all samples. Earlier, we converted that distance into real-variable terms, put it on either side of the observed sample value, and rejected the null hypothesis if the resulting interval did not reach as far as zero. Here, in the final algebraic step above, we reject the null hypothesis if the sample value is more than the critical distance away from 0. This shows that the interval-estimation approach and the direct approach to significance testing use precisely the same decision rule; they simply arrive at it by a different mode of thinking. The first approach establishes a 95% (or other) interval around the sample value and notes whether the hypothesized population parameter is inside that interval; the second establishes a not-to-be-exceeded distance between sample value and hypothesized population parameter on the basis of 5% (or other) risk of type I error.

It is conceptually reassuring to see that we can establish a critical value for $(\bar{Y}_2 - \bar{Y}_1)$, in this case ±4.89. That is, it is meaningful in the terms in which the research is framed to know that if the sample difference in mean tolerance scores between the two groups is greater than 4.89 in absolute magnitude, the hypothesis of no relationship in the population can be rejected at the 5% level. In truth, this is slightly more trouble than researchers usually take. It will do just as well to calculate t on the basis of the observed sample results and note whether it is beyond the critical value found from the table, in this case ±1.98. That is true because the above series of algebraic steps shows that if t is beyond ±1.98 (given our subsample sizes and variances), then $(\bar{Y}_2 - \bar{Y}_1)$ will automatically be beyond ±4.89, and vice versa. We can use the two bases interchangeably. In our illustrative example, the t that would be calculated from the sample data given, using the above definition of t, is $t = -14 / 2.47 = -5.67$, which surely far exceeds in absolute magnitude the required critical value of −1.98. On this basis, we would reject the hypothesis of a zero population parameter at the 5% level.

This approach is especially handy in the age of computers. Instead of outputting hundreds of *different* critical values (comparable to 4.89) for all the different relationships that might be under consideration, each of which must then be compared to the obtained sample values for those particular relationships, the computer merely gives the calculated values of t in each case, all of which, if the operative sample size does not change, are to be compared to the *same* criterion, or critical value, for example, ±1.98. In fact, investigators frequently simply become sensitive to the rounded value "2," and use it when there is reason to want to scan a large number of *t* values or *Z* values rather quickly for the interest they may hold.

As a final note in this section, let us consider the factors that determine whether a result will be statistically significant. We can do this best by considering the *t* statistic itself, keeping in mind that the larger the *t*, the smaller the significance level, that is, the more resoundingly the null hypothesis is rejected. The factors that determine significance duplicate those that determined the size of confidence intervals, with one important addition. There, we pointed first to the worst-case or error level selected. The same applies here; it is obviously easier to get a statistically significant result at the 10% or 20% level than at the 5% or 1% level. The calculated value of *t* would not change, but the critical value in the table with which we compare it would differ. In practice, the convention that centers on the 5% level as a maximum greatly restricts one's latitude for affecting the outcome of the test by manipulating the significance level. In addition, the next section will show that significance levels are often not selected ahead of time anyway.

Second, the subsample variances, and therefore the population subgroup variances, are clearly a factor: the larger the variances, the larger the denominator of *t*, and therefore the smaller the *t* statistic altogether. Significant results are thus more likely when variances are small. Surely, this makes sense. If the population variances are small, the samples will quite accurately reflect the population values. Thus, we can say with relatively great confidence (small chance of error) whether the population parameter is zero or not.

The third factor, again just as in the case of confidence intervals, is the sample sizes. The larger the subsample sizes, the smaller the denominator of *t*, and therefore the larger the *t* altogether. Again, this makes perfect sense: Large samples are very accurate ones, and one should be able to say on the basis of a very large sample, with little chance of error, just what the population parameter is, and in particular whether it is zero or not. Sample size is in fact crucial. Since one has little control over significance levels or population variances, sample size emerges once more as the most obvious way to affect the results of classical statistical inference. In fact, with sample sizes of 500 or 1,000, *almost any sample relationship will be statistically significant*, and the test loses its usefulness. True, with large samples that show a nonzero relationship, even if it be a very small one, we can be confident that the null hypothesis is not true, but it means little or nothing to reject the null hypothesis when the magnitude of the true population parameter may be very puny indeed. Who cares about puny relationships?

This brings us to the last of the factors that affect significance, and probably the most important. This is the magnitude of the relationship in the sample, which reflects the magnitude of the *true* population parameter. The larger the sample difference-of-means, for example, the larger the numerator of t, and therefore the larger the t altogether. Again, this makes perfect sense. It is in fact the direct mathematicization of the logic of significance testing: The more distant the sample value is from zero, the more confidence we have in rejecting the hypothesis that the population parameter is zero. Significance testing is made, in a sense, to reflect strength of relationship: We are pleased to be able to reject at the .01 or .001 level because it suggests that our sample relationship must really be strong. Of course, such results might only reflect a huge sample size, but if the sample size is moderate, we frequently look to significance testing to tell us something about strength. Obviously, interval estimation is a better way, and everybody knows and says that it should be used more, but it is more trouble. For better or worse, significance testing is vastly more common, at least outside of economics. The final section of the monograph will take up significance testing as an indicator of strength of relationship in greater detail.

The Textbook versus the Informal Approach

What has just been presented in this section is what might be called the "textbook" method of directly testing the significance of a sample value. One establishes a risk of error ahead of time; that is, one decides on the .05 level of significance, or the .01 level, or the .001, and so on. One then rejects the null hypothesis or not on the basis of whether the t value calculated with the sample data falls beyond the preestablished critical value of t corresponding to that probability. In our case, we rejected the null hypothesis at the .05 level because the sample t, −5.67, was beyond the critical t of −1.98.

There is a variant of the textbook method that is not really legitimate, strictly speaking, but that is in fact more common. In this variant, one looks at one's sample results first, before establishing a critical value. This would seem to be cheating, and, in a way, it is. In fact, in this variant a critical value is never really established. One merely notes a value of t that is exceeded by the sample result, usually the largest exceeded t value in the table for the relevant degrees of freedom (farthest out in tails), and reports that the results are significant at the probability level corresponding to that t — the .05 level, the .01, level .001, or whatever. Otherwise, the results are reported as "nonsignificant," usually meaning not statistically significant at the .05 level. In our case, for example, the sample t being −5.67, the results might be reported as significant at the .001 level, which is as far as our t table goes. That makes the result look good — the null hypothesis is resoundingly rejected. "Significant at the .001 level" by this method, however, does not equate to a .001 risk of error. Since one has not committed oneself to a decision rule, and is not in fact going to make a decision but only report a "significance" level, there really is no risk of error at all.

This method is responsible for the common sort of table that shows a great many relationships, with various ones marked with one, two, or three asterisks. The footnotes then indicate that one asterisk means $p < .05$, or the 5% level, two mean $p < .01$, or the 1% level, and so on (the p here stands for probability of exceeding, or of error, assuming the truth of the null hypothesis). The purist would discourage this practice. I sympathize with the purist position to a great extent because I believe that the practice tends to make students forget the true meaning of the significance test and the logical procedure that underlies it. On the other hand, the more practical view might be to judge on the basis of whether, in last analysis, the claims being made for the *real-world* (rather than statistical) significance of the results are overblown or are reasonable, regardless of whether the textbook method was strictly applied.

Two matters have so far been bypassed in this chapter in the interest of continuity of the narrative. The first is that the statistic given above for the difference-of-means as having the t distribution actually has the t distribution only when the sample sizes are large, say greater than 40 in each subgroup. Otherwise, other denominators must be used (with the same numerator) in order for the sampling distribution of the resulting statistic to approximate the t distribution (see Hays, 1981:283-287). The second matter concerns the sort of error we sought to minimize; it is not the only sort of error that counts.

Type II Error

The label "Type I" error implies that there must be other types, and there is indeed a "Type II" error that may be extremely important. We concern ourselves with Type I error most commonly because holding that value to some small number generally forces an appropriately difficult criterion upon the investigator. We are forcing the investigator to be appropriately conservative. If we allowed the significance level to be commonly set at .50 instead of .05, we would be giving investigators a 50-50 chance of being able to reject the null hypothesis even if it were true. Generally speaking, we like to be more conservative than that; we want to allow ourselves to be persuaded that a relationship exists in a population only if the evidence is quite compelling, that is, if the sample value observed is quite distant from zero.

If the investigator were trying to persuade us that a relationship actually is zero or near zero, however, the opposite would be true. In such a case, the null hypothesis is not a straw-man claim, but a truly held hypothesis about the world. To demand conservatism and remain somewhat hard to persuade, one would want to minimize the probability of failing to reject the null hypothesis, which is what the investigator now wants us to do, when it is actually false. That is the definition of Type II error. Thus, Type I error means error committed by rejecting the null hypothesis (when it is true), whereas Type II error means error committed by accepting the null hypothesis (when it is false).

Concern for Type II error can arise in many sorts of cases — whenever there is a legitimate concern about missing a true relationship (or univariate value) by being too quick to accept a null hypothesis. One of the most common sorts of occasion in social research relates to program evaluation (Julnes and Mohr, 1989). Sometimes, one wants to show that a policy or program is unnecessary, or is not being effective, or would not be harmful. One might want to show, for example, that regular police patrols do not prevent crime, or that a negative income tax does not reduce work incentives, or that a certain food additive does not increase the risk of cancer in rats. In such cases, we might want to hold on to the notion that the programs or policies really do make an important difference unless the investigator can show us a sample value that is quite close to zero, that is, one that shows the policy as making very little difference indeed. We want to minimize the chance of accepting the null hypothesis in error.

Unfortunately, the statistics connected with hypothesis testing when the primary concern is with Type II error are more complicated, demanding extended treatment in themselves (see Cohen, 1987; Hays, 1981). The present monograph would exceed its stipulated length and level of difficulty by including such a treatment here. I say "unfortunately," however, because this topic is an important one and, for such reasons as I have just given, the typical course in statistics and many elementary textbooks also omit it altogether, or give it almost no emphasis.

One element may be noted, even though a thorough treatment is not possible here. In order to know the probability of error in failing to reject a null hypothesis (or any hypothesis) when it is false, it is necessary to have some assumption about what is true. Assume, for example, that the null hypothesis about the population is false. A sample difference-of-means that is nevertheless very small, thus perhaps leading to acceptance of the null hypothesis in error, is much more likely to occur when the true population difference is small than when it is very large. Thus, in worrying about the *probability* of Type II error, the investigator will in general have to decide on some *maximum tolerable relationship* and make a working assumption that such a relationship exists in the population. In this fashion, accepting a null hypothesis really becomes a matter of rejecting a population relationship of a certain magnitude or greater — a very healthy, meaningful procedure.

It is difficult to justify the lopsided emphasis on Type I error found in social research. This is true not only because a legitimate concern for Type II error is far more widespread than we tend to recognize in practice, but also because the above logic of dealing with Type II error can put a healthy perspective on dealing with Type I error, as well. In particular, this logic suggests that we should not always test the hypothesis of zero relationship when we want to establish that a relationship probably does exist. Rejecting a claim of precisely zero is, after all, not very informative. Instead, we should put ourselves in the position of saying, "I believe that there is a relationship in the population of at least such-and-such a magnitude," and then test and hope to reject the hypothesis that it is smaller. A statistically significant result in such a case would then be meaningful; it would tend to convey substantive significance, as well as statistical.

Technically speaking, such a procedure is only a minor modification of the one that is commonly used. Practically speaking, however, it would be a lot of trouble; it would force the investigator to think about and supply meaningful numbers to computer programs, and it would necessitate that computer programs *ask* the user for such numbers instead of automatically throwing zero into the formula for t. (In fact, the common practice long predated computers; I am only suggesting that the age of computers has reinforced it.) There is little likelihood that such an amount of trouble will be commonly taken in the near future. I have included this brief discussion nevertheless in the belief that an understanding of significance testing requires this particular perspective on its limitations.

One-Tailed Tests

The point just made provides a natural introduction to the subject of one- and two-tailed tests in that it raises the issue: "Which null hypothesis shall I test and try to reject?" Up to the previous paragraph, no mention was made of testing any null hypothesis for bivariate statistics except the hypothesis that a population parameter is zero. Yet, the null hypothesis of precisely zero is in fact not the only one that is commonly tested. A slight variant of it is also quite prevalent to accommodate one-tailed testing, and the t tables are generally modified a bit to allow for this option.

We have not up to now explored the general question of how one *decides* which hypothesis to test as the "null" hypothesis — zero, non-zero, or what have you. The proper answer is to test the hypothesis that is the opposite, or complement, of what one might call the "research" hypothesis — the hypothesis that the investigator is interested in supporting as a conclusion of the testing procedure. If the research hypothesis is that a relationship exists in the population, then the proper null hypothesis is that the population parameter is zero. That is the opposite of "exists." If the research hypothesis is that a relationship of less than –5 exists in the population, an example of the sort of procedure suggested at the end of the previous section, then the proper null hypothesis is that the population parameter is –5 or greater.

Tests of the null hypothesis that a parameter expressing a relationship is equal to some specific number other than zero are very rare. It is not so rare at all, however, to test the null hypothesis that the parameter is greater than or equal to zero, or less than or equal to zero, rather than precisely zero itself. Let us systematize that testing procedure a bit to show this by listing four steps:

1. Establish a "test" or "null" hypothesis, H_0, by taking the opposite, or complement, of the research hypothesis.

2. Select a percentage risk of error, call it "alpha %," of rejecting H_0 when it is true (Type I error).

3. Establish a "critical region" of the t (or other) distribution, bounded on the near side by the critical value(s). The region beyond the critical value(s) must

be such as to contain the least probable alpha % of all sample t, assuming the null hypothesis to be true.

    4. Reject H_0 if the observed sample t falls in the critical region.

Up to now, we have conformed to the above steps in the following fashion. Let us assume a research hypothesis stating that some relationship between ambition and tolerance exists in the population. Step 1 directs us to establish the null hypothesis by taking the opposite. The opposite of "some relationship exists" is "no relationship exists," that is, the measure of the relationship is zero.

Proceeding to step 2, let us opt for a 5% risk of error in rejecting the null hypothesis when it is true. In step 3, we then establish a critical region containing the least probable t, given the truth of the null hypothesis, such that all together they amount to 5% of the total. No matter what value is assumed for the population parameter in calculating t from sample data, the *most* probable t under that assumption is always zero, since the most probable sample relationship would duplicate the population relationship, making the numerator of the t statistic zero. Thus, the least probable t are the furthest away from zero. At 120 degrees of freedom, the critical value is the double value ±1.98, since these t values mark off a critical region containing the most distant 2.5% in each tail (see Figure 5.1). Step 4 then directs us to reject H_0 if the sample t is greater than 1.98 or less than −1.98.

It would in fact be rare, however, to have a research hypothesis that is so noncommittal. If one suspects a relationship between two variables, one generally has some idea of why it would exist, and therefore would expect it to be either positive or negative, and not just nonzero. For example, if my thinking and prior research lead me to suspect a relationship between ambition and tolerance, that same thinking is likely to leave me with a belief about its direction. I might, for example, believe that ambition depresses tolerance, so that the expected relationship is negative (the higher the ambition, the lower the tolerance). Under these circumstances, it is still possible to follow through the above four steps, but the results are a bit different.

    1: My research hypothesis now states that the population relationship is negative. The opposite of a negative relationship is a relationship of zero or greater. The latter, then, becomes the null hypothesis.

    2: Let us again risk 5% chance of error.

    3: What region contains the least probable 5% of all possible sample t, assuming the null hypothesis to be true? In this case, the null hypothesis is that the relationship is zero *or greater*. The trick in one-tailed testing is that we can work with the single t distribution in which the population parameter is assumed to be zero while testing the composite null hypothesis that it is zero or greater. If the population parameter is in reality zero, then the most probable sample relationship is zero. If we also *assume* the population parameter to be zero and plug that value into the formula for t, then the numerator of the most probable t statistic will be $0 - 0$, or $t = 0$. If the population parameter is in reality greater than zero, however, then the most probable sample relationships will also be positive in sign. If we do not change the *assumption* in that circumstance, *the numerator of t would then most probably be positive* (some positive sample value minus the assumed zero). In the case of this composite null hypothesis, then, as long as zero is assumed and plugged in for the parameter, all positive values of t must be considered to be probable, and no positive values improbable. If the null hypothesis that the parameter is zero or greater were really true, the only really improbable t would be negative t, and 5% of all possible t that are the most improbable under these composite conditions are the 5% of all possible t that are the most negative (i.e., further to the left in the t distribution). In other words, the critical region is concentrated entirely in the negative tail, rather than being divided between the two tails (see Figure 5.2). This means that we would reject the null hypothesis (zero or positive) and accept our research notion that a negative relationship exists in the population only if the sample yields a strong negative relationship, which of course makes excellent sense.

How negative? That is, what value of t marks off the 5% negative tail? This may easily be read from the table (still assuming 120 degrees of freedom), where we see that, whereas $t = -1.98$ would mark off the most negative 2.5%, it is $t = -1.658$ that marks off the most negative 5%. Our critical value at the 5% level for a one-tailed test of a hypothesis of negative relationship is therefore $t = -1.658$.

4: Any t that is less than -1.658 therefore directs rejection of the null hypothesis. If the hypothesized relationship had been positive in the first place, of course, then the null hypothesis would have stipulated zero or less, and the critical region would have been entirely concentrated in the positive tail.

Since most hypotheses by far are directional, most significance testing should be one-tailed testing, but in fact it is not. Investigators frequently (not always, by any means) use two-tailed testing, even when their idea is that the population relationship is positive (or negative).

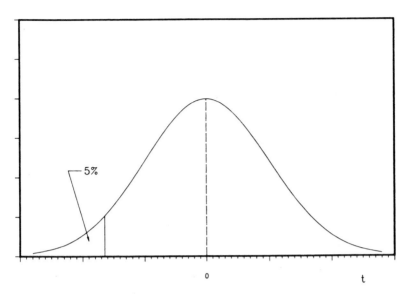

Figure 5.2. A One-Tailed *t* Test

What this means in effect is that they are being even more conservative than it seems; when testing at the 5% level, they are really testing at the 2.5% level, since values in only one of the tails would lead them to reject the null hypothesis and offer the sample results as support for their original beliefs. The same is true of the informal approach described above. One asterisk and a footnote indicating significance at the 5% level would truly mean, in many cases, "If I had used an a priori decision rule of 2.5% with a one-tailed test, this result would have been statistically significant." The claimed .05 level is therefore a show of modesty; the investigator could have claimed significance for the results at the .025 level.

6. THE FUNCTIONS OF THE TEST

Having probed the technical meaning of the significance test, it remains to explore its substantive meaning — what it tells us about the world. The univariate case is quite clear. We can test the null hypothesis that the mean income in a population is, say, $20,000, and either reject it or not on the basis of the mean income in a random sample. Significance testing is primarily used with bivariate and multivariate statistics, however; that is, it is used to say something about relationships. Here, the picture is not so clear; it is clouded by the issue of causality and by the use of ambiguous terms such as "real." I suggest that a measure of clarity can be introduced by consideration of four functions of the test. These are definitely not the only ways in which the significance test is used, but they do cover a very large proportion of common practice. The four are the survey-design function, the experimental-design function, the econometric-modeling function, and the strength-of-relationship function (see Mohr, 1988:90-96).

By the "function" of a test, I mean the kind of information that the significance test gives when interpreted in conjunction with the design and data-analysis operations employed. In order to discuss the functions of significance tests, it is important to keep in mind the meaning of the fundamental concept of a sampling distribution. The sampling distribution is valuable to know about because, under a given set of particular assumptions about the population, it tells us what the probabilities are of getting any specific value (or set of values) when sampling from that population. It is also important to bear in mind that the idea of known sampling distributions applies only under conditions of random sampling; statisticians have essentially nothing to say about the probability of one value or another when the sampling is not fundamentally random.

The first function of significance testing, and the one we have presumed all along, is called the *survey-design* function. It might also rather loosely be called the *population-inference* function to distinguish it from the causal-inference function, to be reviewed below. Here, the test yields the probability of getting a sample statistic — a difference between two means, let us say — beyond a certain magnitude when sampling at random from a population in which the comparable value (difference-of-means) is zero. For example, if we assume that the difference in mean tolerance is zero between those people in the population who are ambitious and those who are unambitious, the significance test informs us about the probability of getting a large difference of means, even so, in a random sample. If we do get an improbably large difference, we would then tentatively reject the notion that the population value is truly zero, since this was only a hypothesis and not an observation.

Note that we would not be in a position to say that the levels of ambition *caused* the levels of tolerance; many other explanations for the difference-of-means are possible. Here, the maxim that "correlation does not imply causation" becomes an important caveat. Variables can be correlated in the world without one causing the other at all. In particular, they may be correlated in a given population simply by coincidence. In a specific five-year period, for example, it may rain quite a bit toward the beginning of the week and hardly at all toward the end, but no causality is necessarily involved, that is, day of the week does not cause rain. Presumably, if we looked at a 100-year period the correlation would disappear. However, we do not always have the capability of observing such large chunks of time, or of space. Also, correlations may be "spurious," that is, they may be occasioned entirely, or at least partly, by extraneous forces. For example, the correlation between ambition and tolerance might be due in part to factors of childhood socialization summed up in the concept "birth order": First children may on the whole tend to become both ambitious and intolerant, whereas second or middle children become both less ambitious and more tolerant. To the extent that this spuriousness prevails, ambition itself is not the cause of degree of tolerance.

All we can infer from the test when using a random sample from a large population in this fashion is either that the relationship in the population is probably nonzero or that a zero relationship cannot be rejected. *Why* the population relationship is zero or nonzero is another question. Of course, if one thing causes another in the world, then the two are going to be related to one another somewhere. Thus, establishing that a relationship does or does not exist is at least relevant to the idea of causality. It is important to keep in mind, however, that the amount of causal information the test conveys in itself is quite limited. In short, we use the survey-design function when we have a true interest in the magnitude of relationships in a specific population and do not have the capability of observing the whole population. Typically, once that sort of fact is established the research task has barely begun; the tough and interesting part comes in figuring out why the relationship has the particular magnitude that was observed.

The second function of significance testing is called the *experimental-design* function, or the *causal-inference* function. Whereas one is not able to infer a causal connection in the first kind of case, one can do so in this one. The difference lies in the kind of design that backs up the test. Here, one selects a group, *all* of which is to be observed, and randomly subdivides it into subgroups. This process is generally called "randomization." For example, if we were vitally interested in the effect of a college education on tolerance, we might randomize a group of high school graduates into two subgroups and make one subgroup go through four years of college while not allowing the other to attend. Clearly, we would be very unlikely to be able to accomplish such a design in the world. I chose the example in order to illustrate the point that randomized experiments are not very available to social researchers in real-world settings. If we wish to know the effects of college on tolerance, we simply may not be able to use a design that permits a reliable causal inference. There are exceptions, however. Experimental designs are prevalent in program evaluation; they are also prevalent in laboratory research in psychology, although laboratory research does not always reflect the "real world" very well.

Let us assume for simplicity that the randomization subdivides the group into two subgroups, although one might randomize into more groups, as well. Note that, still thinking of tolerance as an outcome, the mean tolerance in the population from which both of the subsamples were drawn is clearly the same because each subsample was drawn at random from the same "population," namely, just the combined set of subjects before the randomization took place. The population difference-of-means, then, is already known and does not have to be inferred by significance testing or interval estimation; it is just plain zero. Thus, and this is the important implication, the two subgroups can differ in their mean tolerance levels just after the randomization only by the vagaries, generally quite small, of this random sampling process.

One then administers an experimental treatment to one of the two groups. Assume, for example, that one group is sent to college and kept there while the other — the control group — is prevented from attending. Now, we measure tolerance levels after four years of college. Knowing the details of the sampling distribution of the difference-of-means of two random samples from the same population, that is, when the null hypothesis is known to be true, one is now able to say how probable is a difference-of-means of a certain magnitude as a result of the vagaries of the randomization alone. *That is precisely the information communicated by a significance test.* Thus, we know just how probable it is that these two subgroups differed at the outset by any amount in their initial tolerance levels or in any other preexisting causes of later tolerance scores — *all such traits are randomized.* If the significance test tells us that the difference actually observed in the end is improbably large for a randomization vagary, then some of that difference, at least, may with substantial confidence be attributed to the treatment, *since that is the only nonrandomized difference between the two subgroups.* (Of course, it is not the only possible difference; some differences might have crept in after the randomization due to impurities in the way the experiment was conceptualized and carried out. Such "contamination" is always possible, but there are times when we are willing to consider it quite unlikely to be large.)

Note that the conclusion is possible only if there has been randomization, or, let us say, only if there has been an assignment procedure so close to random sampling that the statistical model becomes essentially relevant. The sampling distribution is known only for the case of random sampling, not for the selection of groups or subgroups in just any old way. We might compare two groups of high school graduates that seem to be pretty much the same, but that is not tantamount to randomization. There is in general very little basis for running a significance test on the emerging difference between such groups and making a causal inference; they could have differed in many undetected but important ways right from the beginning. The point is that if one has not randomized, one never knows. If one compared a college group and a noncollege group without randomization or random sampling of any sort, a significance test would have very little apparent relevance (it does rule out such factors as random measurement error). It does not permit a causal inference because of the absence of randomization and it does not permit inference to a larger population because no such population has been randomly sampled.

In the experiment, however, the combination of randomization, a postrandomization administration of the treatment conditions, and a known sampling distribution allows a *causal* inference to be made on the basis of the results of a significance test. The causal conclusion then holds at least for the subjects, times, and conditions observed. Even though one cannot generalize to other individuals and conditions, however, when the design is applicable, it is certainly very powerful. Unfortunately, as noted, most social researchers outside of experimental psychology cannot aspire to conduct randomized experiments on their social and behavioral questions.

The third function is loosely called the "econometric-modeling" function. It is not entirely rare or unusual outside of economics, but it is a common perspective primarily in that discipline. It gives the probability that a parameter estimate of a certain magnitude might be attributable to the random-disturbance component of a model rather than indicating a true causal effect. It is difficult to appreciate the econometric-modeling function without some reliance on the statistical technique called "regression analysis," but a skeletal outline may be provided here.

Consider, for example, that one has assumed that tolerance is caused only by a certain set of specified variables, including ambition among them, plus a random-disturbance component. In other words, we presume that any person's score on the outcome variable (tolerance) is fully determined by our set of causes, except that, for each individual, some positive or negative number picked at random out of a hat (that is, generated at random by other forces in life not included in the analysis) is added to this determined score.

We do not pick a random sample from a larger population nor do we implement any randomization process. We simply observe a collectivity. When one collects data on the variables and analyzes them, a certain relationship will show up between tolerance and ambition, as well as between tolerance and each of the other causes included. The point is that the disturbances meted out to any subgroup are assumed to be a random sample of the population of disturbances. Thus, if ambition itself has absolutely no effect on tolerance, the average tolerance scores of the ambitious and unambitious subgroups should differ only as the result of this random sampling of the disturbances. Do they differ by so much that two random samples from the same population of disturbance scores are unlikely to be responsible? The significance test gives us *precisely* that information. When one tests the relationship between tolerance and ambition for significance, one learns whether (a) it is so large that it probably could not be entirely the misleading result of the random disturbances but indicates, rather, a true causal impact, or (b) it is so small that it might well be due to the random-disturbance component, so that ambition may no longer be assumed to be causal.

Thus, there is a causal inference connected with this function. However, the validity of the causal inference based on the significance test does depend on the validity of the *model*; that is, if the assumption about the specified set of causes is wrong, and there is a cause of tolerance score that is not included in the analysis, then the basis for the causal inference evaporates. That is true because we can no longer pretend that all that is omitted is a *random* disturbance, one that is not related to any of the included predictors. An actual cause has been omitted, and if it is related to ambition, for example (as birth order would be), its absence will magnify the difference in tolerance scores between the ambitious and the unambitious subgroups. That ruins the basis for our causal inference about ambition. In order for the econometric-modeling function to apply, therefore, the model must be correct, that is, every true cause must be included, to the point where all that is left out is a random disturbance. Unfortunately, the models we deal with most are woefully far from this ideal; they leave a lot about the result or dependent variable to be explained, and there is no good basis for assuming that the large portion yet to be explained is random, that is, quite unrelated to the causes already included.

The fourth function is the *strength-of-relationship* function. Researchers hardly ever acknowledge that they are using a significance test in this manner, and this function is not commonly referred to in published material. Yet, it is probably the most common use of all. It is one way that almost all producers and consumers of statistical analyses alike have of assessing quickly, as a first impression, what to make of a reported relationship or a bit of computer output. What it does is to provide a metric of strength of relationship, one that is probably more broadly applicable than any other. It is appealing partly because some strength measures say little in their own voices. What, for example, does a difference-of-means of −14 mean in the case of ambition and tolerance — is this a strong relation, or a weak one, or is it moderate? Even when they do convey a message intrinsically, it is most convenient to be able to translate them all into a common language, whether originally expressed as correlation coefficients, regression coefficients, gammas, taus, chi-squares, or differences-of-means, or whether the measurement scales were dollars, pounds, attitude points, test scores, population densities, or anything else. The terminology for this common language is based in probability. No matter what design or nondesign has been employed, the results of the test give the probability that one would have obtained a statistic in a certain range of magnitude *if* one had actually implemented a randomization or random sampling procedure (given the sample size and variance estimates that were obtained). Any nonsignificant result means that the relationship tested is so small (no matter what its raw magnitude happens to be) that it could fairly easily occur through the vagaries of a randomization or random sampling process. Simple random assignment, for example, would yield a difference-of-means that great more than five times out of a hundred; such a difference-of-means, the test result tells us, is not a remarkably rare event even when looking at the difference between two random samples from the very same population. It therefore may be too small a relationship to bother about even if it were truly causal. In fact, any time, in any research, that a relationship turns out to be nonsignificant statistically, one might, with some caution, interpret it as indicating lack of importance. The basis for such a conclusion would be that if the magnitude of a relationship is such that it could easily occur by a random selection process, it is too puny to repay the time and effort necessary to think about or research it further (Blalock, 1960:270-271). The note of caution referred to is of course necessitated by the possibility that the relationship might be quite strong in some *other* group or subgroup — even a subgroup of the very group observed.

On the other hand, if a relationship is statistically significant, it means that it is so large that it could not easily have occurred as the result of random forces alone. Here, caution is necessary because of sample size; since almost any small relationship will still be statistically significant with very large samples, this interpretation of the test is helpful only with sample sizes in the small to moderate range. If not the result of a random process, why then did the observed magnitude occur? We do not know from the test alone. The relationship may be causal, but it may also be spurious or coincidental (see Mohr, 1988:178-182). We simply know that it is fairly large in this one universal metric. Or, one may compare two relationships with one another that are not otherwise directly comparable (a difference-of-means of 14 attitude points and 638 dollars, for example, or a difference-of-means of 14 and a correlation coefficient of .31). Given roughly similar sample sizes, if one result is barely significant at the .05 level and the other is significant beyond the .001 level, the second may be considered stronger than the first, at least as a starting point for further thought. Of course, there are pitfalls in such thinking; one cannot be a slave to significance tests. But as a first approximation to what is going on in a mass of data, it is difficult to beat this particular metric for communication and versatility.

Thus, common significance tests rank as a first-rate tool for detecting causality in conjunction with randomization designs. They are also convenient in surveys for noting whether population relationships are probably either zero or nonzero, although such information in itself is rather minimal. Survey-design functions and causal-inference do not apply, however, when one has simply observed one or more collectivities of interest — *without* true random sampling or random sampling assumptions — and such studies are probably the most common variety. In such cases, the strength-of-relationship function is the only one of the above that applies. It is a rough tool, but, for most of us, a welcome one.

REFERENCES

BLALOCK, H. (1960) Social Statistics. New York: McGraw-Hill.

COHEN, J. (1987) Statistical Power Analysis for the Behavioral Sciences (rev. ed.). New York: Academic Press.

FISHER, R.A. and YATES, F. (1948) Statistical Tables for Biological, Agricultural and Medical Research. Edinburgh and London: Oliver & Boyd.

HAYS, W. L. (1981) Statistics (3rd ed.). New York: CBS College Publishing.

JULNES, G. and MOHR, L. B. (1989) "Analysis of no-differences findings in evaluation research." Evaluation Review 13(6) pp. 499-525.

MOHR, L. B. (1988) Impact Analysis for Program Evaluation. Chicago: Dorsey.

RUGG, H. O. (1917) Statistical Methods Applied to Education. Boston: Houghton Mifflin.

ABOUT THE AUTHOR

LAWRENCE B. MOHR is Professor of Political Science and Public Policy in the Department of Political Science and the Institute of Public Policy Studies at the University of Michigan. His teaching fields are organization theory, program evaluation, statistics, and the philosophy of social research. He maintains a research and publishing interest in each of these areas.

NOTES

NOTES

NOTES

NOTES